Star

IN YOUR OWN
LIFE STORY

Praise for Star in Your Own Life Story

"An irresistible, brilliant masterpiece! Bravo, two thumbs up and encore! The word "book" doesn't do Amy's creative genius any justice. This is more than a book; it's an indulgent, captivating experience that woos you into a wonderful place that's psychologically stimulating as it takes you on a movie marathon in your mind. You will be swept off your feet and finally able to view your life from a perspective that makes sense, dazzles and dares you to rewrite your story, take center stage and own it! You'll feel every word and the light bulbs will pop on as you reminisce and re-discover your inner wisdom and strength. *Star In Your Own* Life Story will caress your soul, stir your senses and awaken the power within so you can step from behind the curtain, own your leading role, and shine like the star you already are."

—**Catrice M. Jackson**, Speaker, BOSSLady of Branding
& Brand Message Mentor www.catriceology.com

"Think Self-Help meets Hollywood, as Amy's book takes the reader on a magical ride using metaphors from famous movie characters to help nudge you forward in your life to be the brilliant person you were always meant to be."

—**Sherry Gaba**, LCSW, Speaker, Author of The Law of
Sobriety, CBS radio Host www.sherrygaba.com

"Amy O'Brien asks a life-changing question in her new book, *Star in Your Own Life Story*: What if your life were a movie? Her inspiration to live the life you choose is contagious. Read the book and catch this playful way of looking at your life. It's transformation the easy-going, fun way."

—**Lynnet McKenzie**
www.OpeningtoEcstasy.com

"Amy has done a wonderful job of making personal development entertaining! I loved how she took fairy tales we all grew up with, compared them to their newer "updated" versions, and brought to our attention the lessons to learn in them. We so often watch a good movie for their entertainment value alone, failing to see, or even more yet, teach our children these lessons. I was enlightened with some very thought provoking topics where I took notice and contemplated issues in my own life. I loved the 'what if' questions in Step two: "Who in their right mind would marry someone after a single dance?" "Wouldn't we be offended if a man could only identify us by our shoe size?" I laughed out loud at that last one! Any woman could read this book and relate to the characters, see lessons to be learned, and put them into practice in her own life. A great read for anyone looking to discover how to be the star in her own life story!"

—**AMY J THORESON**, Author & Entrepreneur, *Discovering Life's Blessings in Disguise*, Co-Author of *A Juicy Joyful Life*

Star in Your Own Life Story takes us on a delightful journey using popular filmography like the *Wizard of Oz* to demonstrate how we can overcome obstacles, achieve our dreams, and evolve into our magnificent selves. Amy demonstrates how to bring our powerful life stories to to world, one act at a time.

—**SHANN VANDER LEEK**, Transformation Goddess and creator of the *Sacred Heart Teachings* www.ShannVanderLeek.com

"I've read hundreds of personal development books and *Star in Your Own Life Story* guides and entertains in a most magical way. Who new that all I needed to do was watch the *Wizard of Oz* for lessons in personal growth and transformation! Author Amy O'Brien's writing is authentic as she shares her expertise in personal development practices, love of the movies and her soul. If you want to be engaged, entertained and enriched, this book will nourish you page by page."

—**DR MADISEN HARPER**, #1 International Bestselling Author of *limitLESS – 10 Energy* Excelerators *to Access Your Infinite Potential*

"Amy drills down to the core of the issues we face in life, and provides step by step instruction, showing you how to re-create the movie that is your life. You cannot help but be inspired to make the positive changes you knew you should have been making all along. You'll learn your value, how to overcome your fears, become in tune with the messages of your body, and so much more. You'll be so grateful that you decided to read this book, because you will finally become the star of your life that you have always craved to be."

—**STACY CORRIGAN**, Chief Manifester, Speaker and Author of *Manifest Your Man*®

"I have had the joy of watching the Star in Your Own Life Story system emerge over the past few years...and bravo! Amy has brilliantly blended the movie metaphor with the trials, tribulations and triumphs of life. She's a great storyteller – and if you're going through any kind of challenge you want to find an answer to, this book provides it!"

—**Marcia Bench**, Marcia Bench Enterprises, LLC www.yourdivinegifts.com

Star
IN YOUR OWN
LIFE STORY

Overcome Obstacles,
Achieve Your Dreams, and
Become Your Best Self

AMY BETH O'BRIEN, M.S.

Star in Your Own Life Story: *Overcome Obstacles, Achieve Your Dreams, and Become Your Best Self*

Website for book: http://amybethobrien.com

Published by Bright Red Cardinal Press

ISBN-10: 0615794998
ISBN-13: 978-0-615-79499-0

Front Cover Imagery: Shutterstock.com
Cover Design and Interior Layout: AuthorSupport.com

For Jack and Christopher

Table of Contents

ACKNOWLEDGMENTS

*T*his book is a culmination of years of self-study, personal experience, professional training, and my unwitting attendance in the school of hard knocks. It's interesting to see how seemingly unrelated things are interconnected. This book is where a variety of subjects that I love to talk about, learn about, and benefit from come together like some sort of cosmic puzzle. So I guess my first nod must to go the universe, God, or whatever that helped me to create this. I am both the writer and the subject of this book. I am author and client, teacher and student. They, whoever they are, say that we teach what we most need to learn. I think we all need to learn what's in this book at one time or another. I continue to open its pages and remind myself that its wisdom, because it isn't necessarily mine, is ours.

My boys, Jack and Christopher—you are my family. My hope is that as you go through life and face your own challenges, you will benefit from what I've learned and find comfort and helpful guidance in this book.

My editor, Victoria Wright, whose mastery over the proper use of the hyphen and all things grammatical frees me from my inner perfectionist in order to get my thoughts down on paper.

I'd also like to acknowledge Caroline Myss and Anodea Judith for their wonderful texts on the chakras and archetypes. I absolutely love, and benefit from, their writings and programs.

Maureen Spencer, my very first yoga teacher, who introduced me to energy anatomy. Yoga continues to be a primary way for me to express my talents as a transformational teacher, to tune in to my body's wisdom, and to help others do the same.

Finally, I must thank all of the creative artists out there—the authors, screenwriters, actors, directors, producers, set designers, composers, and everyone who has the courage to be the channel that brings art, entertainment, and powerful stories to the world. It isn't always an easy path, but it's a big part of what gives our lives meaning. Through our own creativity, however we express it and whatever we produce, we all make a little more sense of things, come closer to understanding our purpose, and experience more joy.

INTRODUCTION

Ten Steps to Starring in Your Own Life Story

ACT 1	ACT 2	ACT 3
Challenge	Transformation	Resolution

- Embrace your inner *Screenwriter*
- Develop your *Character*
- Become a *Producer*
- Listen to your *Director*
- Be the *Star*
- Learn your *Lines*
- Find your Supporting *Players*
- Set the *Stage*
- *Edit* your Film
- Accept your *Oscar*

What if Your Life Were a Movie?

*I*magine sitting in a movie theater. You're watching the opening credits, and you're about to be introduced to the protagonist and the conflict and personal challenge she faces. Over the next two hours you're going to bear witness to how she faces and resolves her situation.

The protagonist enters, and much to your surprise, it's you. This is a story from your life, and the opening scene introduces the audience to the current challenge you're facing. It may be your career, your relationships, your home, or yourself. Perhaps it's a dream that goes unfulfilled, or a personal problem that's on your mind—a lot.

If the movie-you continued on the same path that you have been on in real life, would the audience want to stand up and cheer? Would they be impressed by your character? Would they leave the theater totally inspired? Or would they feel the opposite? Would they be bored, frustrated, or even angry? Would they want to walk out of the theater and ask for a refund?

What if your life were a movie?

This is the question I asked myself one day when I was in Target. I was placing my items up on the conveyor belt and thinking about my relationship. It's one whose demise I affectionately refer to as death by a thousand petty annoyances. I won't go into detail about all the things that bothered me about Joe, but suffice it to say that I did what many of us do when we know, deep down, that we're with the wrong person.

I tried to make it work anyway.

That all changed the day I was in Target holding a car scraper.

Joe would insist that the canned goods be placed on the shelves, *Sleeping-with-the-Enemy* style, labels facing the same way out. He would take me to dinner one night and then suggest we eat lunch out the next day but conveniently forget his wallet. It's not that I thought I should never have to pay for anything. It was the passive aggression I had a problem with. He'd leave me in line at the drugstore—with his basketful of items—and wouldn't return until after I'd paid for them. If I told him what his items cost, he'd say, "You're not going to make me pay for those, are you? I took you to dinner last night."

He played on my guilt so that I'd pay for his things, and I was so concerned about rocking the boat that I did it. At the time, I was divorced, my boys were in elementary school and after-school care, and I was living paycheck to paycheck. I did push back, but he'd blame me for picking up the tab. He said that he didn't expect me to pay for his items, and it was my fault if I did. This was basically true, although of course he knew I would. I was allowing him to manipulate me.

That all ended when Joe handed me a twenty-dollar car scraper and walked off. I glanced at the celebrities on the magazine covers, and I had this thought. *What if my life was a movie? Would my audience be frustrated by my character, or would they be inspired?*

I knew they'd be frustrated. I was. I wanted to be the inspiring leading lady, not the victim, and to me, an inspiring leading lady wouldn't keep making the same mistake over and over again. So I wrote a new script that went something like this.

Int. Target, Day

```
Amy places her items up on the belt. She
waits for the cashier to finish with the
customer ahead of her in line, and then
hands her Joe's car scraper.

                    Amy
        I decided I don't want this.

The cashier takes the scraper and places
it behind the counter.

Amy walks out of the store with her shoul-
ders back and her head held high. She takes
a deep breath and can't keep the smile off
her face.

Int. Joe's Apartment


Amy is emptying the shopping bags and put-
ting things away.

                   Joe
         Where's my car scraper?

                   Amy
    Oh, that? When you didn't come back to pay
     for it, I assumed you didn't want it.
```

Joe couldn't argue. He had already said he didn't mean for me to pay for his things (only hold onto them and give them to the cashier to put away, apparently). In Step Six, "Learn Your Lines, Lead with Assertiveness," you'll read more about passive aggression.

Little did I know that that one question, *What if my life was a movie?* would cause my entire life to change.

I had developed a spiritual practice that involved a lot of yoga and meditation which made me feel at peace, but I'd become passive, at least at home. At work, I didn't have a problem standing up for myself. But with Joe, I'd taken on the role of peacekeeper. I was put in the awkward position of not wanting to fight in front of my kids while at the same time not wanting them to think it was okay for a man to ridicule me. It was a no win situation, or so I thought. I knew that if I was ever going to have the kind of relationship I wanted, I'd have to get my voice back. I started to assert myself around him, regardless of how he felt about it, and in spite of how unnatural it felt. Some of the conversations became so absurd that I'd retreat to my computer and write out the dialogue. If I hadn't been living it, it probably would have made for some great comedy.

It wasn't entirely Joe's fault. By failing to play the leading role in my life up until that time, I wound up playing an inauthentic character in his. Perhaps you can relate to feeling as though you're molding yourself to another person's tastes based on how you think they want you to be, instead of trusting that who you are will attract the right partner (job, business, clients, life).

I ended the go-nowhere relationship with him and applied the same view-my-life-as-a-movie process to finding a great new place to live.

Writing a New Script

A year after Joe and I split up, I was overcome with an urge to write. I would walk along the Charles River in Boston during my lunch break from my job as the learning and development director at the Massachusetts Department of Environmental Protection. As I walked, there would be a conversation going on in my head about a time, years before, when I found my ex-husband at another woman's apartment. I'd moved on from that experience, but I couldn't stop thinking about it. Our marriage lasted another two and a half years before we parted ways. Even though they wound up together after we divorced, I still had doubts, and those doubts played over and over in my mind.

It was as though a conversation was constantly taking place in my head among several female characters—the wise woman, the skeptic, the feminist, and the judge. I saw it as a movie, and since I was unable to simply write in my journal about it, I knit instead. I probably produced more hats, scarves, and sweaters in a six month period that I had in the previous ten years.

But the urge to write wouldn't go away. I couldn't understand it. I never saw myself as a writer, other than the writing I did as an instructional designer. But I'd come to believe in my intuitive hunches, so I sat down at the keyboard and began. It was mostly dialogue, and because I saw it as a moving picture, I began to study screenwriting. I learned about the three-act structure of film and how to format of a screenplay, and for the next two years, when I wasn't busy with my job or my boys, I worked on my script. It wasn't an easy task. I questioned what I was doing, and my inner film critic worked hard to try to get me to stop wasting my time. But my inner film director, my wise intuitive guide, urged me to keep going and trust the process.

Stitches became a story about a group of women who meet every Sunday at a yarn shop, and the protagonist, a young mother of two small sons, confides in the group about her husband's possible infidelity. Some of the absurdity from my interactions with Joe worked their way into the script too. By re-working my personal challenge, I was able to resolve it in a way that I was never able to achieve in real life.

I began to wonder if it could ever actually be produced, but I found out that Julia Roberts bought the rights to the *Friday Night Knitting Club* and planned to turn it into a movie, right at the time I finished it. My script consultant said that there'd only be room in Hollywood for one knitting-based movie. I was disappointed, but also a bit awestruck at the same time, because when someone had asked me who I envisioned playing Molly Gardner, the owner of Stitches, I said Julia Roberts.

I knew there was a reason I'd written *Stitches*. Deep down I never really felt it was meant to be made into a movie. I allowed myself to indulge the thought, but I knew there was another purpose for writing it.

Around the time that I finished it, I met Erin Brockovich through a mutual friend. She came to Boston to speak at a conference, and I had the pleasure of sharing a pumpkin martini with her and her husband at the Oak Room. I found it divinely interesting that I should meet the woman whose life story earned Julia Roberts a Best Actress Oscar in 2000.

In the meantime, I applied the same view-my-life-as-a-movie approach to my work life. As the leading character, I wanted to play the part of someone who was happy in her career, so I set about finding a position that took better advantage of my skills and talents and allowed me to work from home, at least some of the time, so that I could spend more time with my boys. I quickly landed a new job as a consultant with Brainshark. I loved what I was doing. For the first time in years, I got to travel and work from home part-time, and my career-coaching, managing, and training background were a perfect fit for the job. My scriptwriting skills came in handy, too, since Brainshark is software that creates web-based, video presentations using PowerPoint, and writing a script is the first step in building one. In addition to helping clients, I wrote tutorials and marketing presentations.

In the fall of 2009 I was again inspired to write. After I wrote *Stiches*, I stopped thinking about that time in my life. I got over it. *That* was my reason for writing it. I knew I had to share this process and everything I'd learned about the power of being the protagonist in your own life and using script writing to overcome personal challenges. The result, nine months later, was *Stuck with Mr. Wrong? Ten Steps to Starring in Your Own Life Story*, which picked up four awards, including an International Book Award for the best self-help relationship book of the year.

One of the women who read it said, "All my life I wondered, where's the book that's supposed to tell me how to navigate my life? This is it!"

And she's happily married with three children.

Another reader, also happily married with three children, came to realize that her frustrations didn't stem from her husband, but from not doing enough for herself.

When I arrived at the NECN (New England Cable News) studios for my first television interview to promote the book, I had no idea what questions I'd be asked. I sat beside Leslie Gaydos, the interviewer, and waited while they introduced our segment, called "Off the Shelf." The producer chose to show the trailer to *Eat Pray Love* as the introduction, since she correctly viewed *Stuck with Mr. Wrong* as a book that takes the reader through a similar, transformational journey. I laughed inside at God's sense of humor, since Julia Roberts starred in the film.

I was so happy that there were two new movies out in 2012 that put a modern twist on Snow White, including Mirror Mirror, starring Julia Roberts. You'll read all about it in Step Two, "Develop Your Character, Lead with Light," along with Pretty Woman, which depicts a modern-day princess who mimics Rapunzel at the end. Eat Pray Love shows a transformation of character that I review in the Star in Your Own Life Story on-line course, which you can learn more about by going to www. STARinYourOwnLifeStory.com/course.

In the interview, Leslie commented that the steps in the book could be applied to any area where you're stuck. And it's true.

Not everyone is stuck with Mr. Wrong, but we all become stuck in our lives in one way or another, whether it has to do with love, work, home, or self. And chances are the "thing" we point to that's keeping us trapped isn't really it. It goes much deeper. It all comes down to your inside story.

This book will help you to identify what's holding you back so that you can step into your starring role as the inspiring lead character in your own life story. For you that could mean removing blocks that have been preventing you from going after your dream of living in the limelight on a literal stage or in your chosen profession. It could mean choosing to take charge at home or to become more assertive in your relationships. Or, it could mean taking an objective look at how you've been living, what you've been pursuing, and realizing that happiness will come from simplifying your life and living a quiet existence. Being a star means having the self-confidence to create a life that feels right to you, establishing your own standards of success, and then creating a life script according to these values. This book will walk you through ten steps that will show you how.

Three Acts to Creating Your Best Life Script

Movies that inspire, the ones we remember, have a main character who undergoes a transformation. In order to resolve the conflict or overcome the challenge which is the focus of the story, she must face certain aspects of herself in three main areas. Her journey will present her with a variety of opportunities where she can choose to face her fears and self-doubts, examine her beliefs, and connect with what's in her heart, or stay stuck in her act 1 challenge.

In this book you will learn how to take center stage as the lead character in your life story. You will learn a ten-step process that follows a movie-making analogy in order to overcome personal challenges, transform your life, and achieve your dreams. I've combined popular films, the three-act structure of movies, filmmaking roles, personal stories, energy anatomy, archetypes, yoga, creative visualization, and writing—all of the things I speak about and teach.

For as many years as you've been alive, you have stories, but there's a reason why certain stories stick around. The ones you remember often contain clues to what's holding you back, as well as to your life purpose.

Storytelling, scriptwriting, and using the power of the personal story as a way to transform your life are what this book is all about.

My favorite childhood film, *The Wizard of Oz*, is full of symbolism and metaphor and provides a blueprint for everything you need in order to overcome personal challenges to find your way *home*. These are illustrated throughout each of the ten steps in this book. Did you ever think about the symbolism behind Dorothy's *ruby* slippers, the *Emerald* city, or the *yellow* brick road? In this book, you'll find out.

Each chapter also contains an overview of another movie with a character transformation that mirrors that particular step and illustrates how every movie, and every personal transformation, contains similar elements that we found with Dorothy.

You'll also learn about the chakra system—seven energy centers of the body. The best way I can think of describing your chakra system is by using stress as an example. Stress is essentially psychological. It takes place in the mind, but it is common knowledge that stress causes illness. Take a look at this fact sheet by the APA and you'll see just how much stress affects health and productivity. http://www.apa.org/practice/programs/workplace/phwp-fact-sheet.pdf

According to the APA, the costs of chronic diseases make up more than 75% of the $2 trillion health care costs in the U.S. Stress causes heart disease, insomnia, headaches, ulcers, and cancer. Think of your chakra system as the connection between your thoughts and feelings and your physical cells. As Caroline Myss, author of Anatomy of the Spirit said, your biography is your biology. Memories, thoughts, and feelings form imprints in your physical body. Balancing your chakras—maintaining a healthy energetic system, is one way of bringing your body back to health. It's also a way to gain insight into an area of your life that you need to work on in order to move ahead.

When I was first introduced to the chakras, I was going through yoga teacher training. Even though I'd had some phenomenal experiences and I'd become more open minded about spirituality and the mysteries of our existence, I was skeptical. The idea that I had an energy body sounded like woo woo, new age b.s. to me. I was resistant to the idea that my life history could cause illness or discomfort in different areas of my body.

At the time, I was a young mother. My boys were both under two. I had overcome anxiety and depression, but still had chronic foot pain. I could no longer do impact sports. Yoga helped me to feel better emotionally, and my foot pain went away. But it wasn't just about the physical exercises, or asanas, as we call them. Something about my yoga practice changed the way I felt mentally and emotionally. It made me feel incredible. My energy picked up, I felt light, and quite happy. As I learned about our chakra system, I understood. Timing my movements with my breath, becoming incredibly focused on the present, and taking time to be still, made me stronger. I became more aware. I grew less willing to live in denial. I became more self-confident.

Each chakra corresponds to a step in this book. You will learn how your thoughts and emotions affect different areas of your body. Taking center stage as the lead character in your own life is not only empowering, but good for your health as well.

Along the way, you will be introduced to archetypes—characters in our collective unconscious who have a major influence on your decision making, thoughts, and behavior.

Acupuncture, acupressure, reiki, tai chi, chi kung, and yoga all work on the energy body. In the on-line course designed to go along with this book, you'll be introduced to a yoga pose designed to help you balance your chakras, along with a brief visualization that will put you in the audience's seat of your movie to imagine a more empowering script for your life. You'll have an opportunity to identify areas where you may feel stuck and to form a strategy for moving ahead.

The Wizard of Oz

When I was a little girl, we had Halloween, Thanksgiving, Christmas, and the *Wizard of Oz*. Because the movie could only be seen once a year, the night the *Wizard of Oz* aired on television felt like a national holiday. The entire day was spent in anticipation and excitement over the big bowl of popcorn your mother was going to make and seeing the MGM lion roar on the tiny screen. It was my favorite childhood movie, but as an adult, I've come to view the picture in a much different way. I love *The Wizard of Oz* because it illustrates so beautifully the three-act process and everything you need to get through your act 2 journey.

In act 1, we are introduced to the protagonist, Dorothy, and her antagonist, Almira Gulch. Toto has apparently bitten Miss Gulch, and she's been given permission to take the dog and have him put down. Toto jumps out of the basket attached to Gulch's bicycle and runs back home, and Dorothy decides that running away is her only option. She sees a fortune teller who sends her back home to Auntie Em as a tornado looms over the horizon. When Dorothy arrives, she's unable to get into the storm cellar, so she goes inside the house, gets knocked over the head when her bedroom window dislodges from its frame, and passes out. She wakes up in a dream world inside the cyclone, where she sees Miss Gulch on her bicycle transform into a witch riding a broomstick. Her house lands right on top of the Wicked Witch of the East, and she finds herself stuck in the world of Oz. Her new challenge is to figure out how to get back home to Kansas.

According to Freud, the characters in our dreams are a manifestation of some aspect of our selves. If we are to look at everything that transpires in Oz from this perspective, then everyone and everything is an outward manifestation of something inside Dorothy. She goes from a world of black and white to color. Dorothy's about to have an awakening of consciousness.

Landing on the Wicked Witch of the East represents Dorothy's desire to have her problem disappear but to remain innocent. She didn't kill the witch, her house landed on her. It was an accident, as Dorothy made sure all the munchkins understood.

It's clear that Dorothy's subconscious mind understands that her problem of Miss Gulch didn't just disappear, and it proves this by manufacturing her sister, the Wicked Witch of the West, who is really Gulch in new form. If we are to look at the witch as an outward manifestation of something inside Dorothy, what she represents is Dorothy's greatest fear: having her power taken away—power to keep her dog, power to control the circumstances of her life.

Throughout the film, Dorothy must constantly deal with the witch. As you recall, the witch's main goal was to get Dorothy to give her the Wicked Witch of the East's ruby slippers, which Glinda, the Good Witch of the North, had placed on Dorothy's feet. In a way, this is symbolic of the fact that Dorothy's power was initially taken from her by Miss Gulch (the Witch of the East). When the ruby slippers are placed on Dorothy's feet, she's taking her power back.

She tells her, "Keep tight inside of them. Their magic must be very powerful, or she wouldn't want them so badly."

By staying in her ruby slippers, Dorothy maintains her ability to stand up to mistreatment or anything else that gets in the way of achieving her vision—in this case, *home*.

Every good movie has an antagonist. The antagonist is the person, place, or situation that presents the greatest obstacle to forward movement. If we are to look at the role of the antagonist from a spiritual perspective, he or she presents the protagonist with the greatest opportunity for growth. In this case, the witch provides Dorothy with the opportunity to face her fears instead of running away.

Glinda, the Good Witch, represents Dorothy's inner wisdom, or her inner film director, which we'll examine in the fourth step to starring in your own life story. She never tells Dorothy how to get home. She guides her down the path of self-discovery—the yellow brick road. And that is the role of the inner director, to guide you to the next step, and then the next. Your job is to take the step with faith, even if you don't know the outcome. Dorothy is off to see the wizard, the wonderful Wizard of Oz.

Along the way, she meets the Scarecrow, Tin Man, and Lion. These three characters not only symbolize our need to gather support around us as we go down our own yellow brick roads, but they represent Dorothy's need to be courageous, keep a positive mindset, and find her true heart's desire.

The first friend she meets is the Scarecrow. She comes to a fork in the road and doesn't know which path to follow. The Scarecrow tells her that either way is fine; in other words, there is no wrong path through life. Every path offers its own set of growth opportunities.

Each new friend is an outward manifestation of Dorothy's self-doubts, or what I like to call her inner film critic. The Tin Man felt he didn't have a heart, the Scarecrow said he didn't have a brain, and the Lion identified himself as a coward.

The witch paints "Surrender Dorothy" across the sky. As a child watching the movie, I thought it meant giving up the ruby slippers, or it was a message for her friends to surrender Dorothy to the witch. Symbolically, it represents Dorothy's need to let go, to not feel as though everything in her life is fully in her control, and to allow the divine to step in.

The Wicked Witch casts a spell upon Dorothy and her friends just as they're about to reach the Emerald City, and they pass out in a field of poppies. This represents Dorothy's desire to give up just as she's about to cross the finish line. But her wise inner director, her intuition, the Good Witch of the North, is there to remind her of the importance of reaching her act 3. She casts a counter-spell to wake them up and put them back on track.

How many times have you wanted to give up on something you've worked so hard for, because you're afraid it's never going to happen—that you're never going to reach the Emerald City, or if you arrive, you'll be disappointed? Like the high school student who drops out in the twelfth grade, you're overcome with an urge to give up. But if you listen to your inner director, you'll find a way to forge ahead.

Dorothy and her friends reach the Emerald City and the wizard tells them to kill the witch and return with her broomstick. When they do, he will give them a heart, a brain, some courage, and an explanation of how to get back home to Kansas. This is symbolic of Dorothy's own acknowledgment that her problems won't go away unless she conquers fear.

Dorothy is eventually kidnapped by the witch, but who/what comes to her rescue? She rescues herself through her intelligence (Scarecrow), her courage (Lion), and her deep, heartfelt desire to go home (Tin Man). It turns out the witch wasn't so powerful. When Dorothy dumps a bucket of water onto the witch, she melts into nothingness.

When the four return to the wizard, the Wicked Witch of the West now gone, and with a broomstick in hand, they discover that the wizard is just a man. The wizard represents Dorothy's desire to look to others for answers, instead of looking within. He is the magic pill. The answers to life's toughest challenges don't come from other people. We know what's right for us, we just need to listen to the voice of our inner wisdom and trust we are being steered in the right direction.

The wizard tells them that they had everything they wanted right inside them all along. The scarecrow had a brain; he just didn't have a diploma. The tin man had a heart, and the lion came to realize that it wasn't courage he lacked, just a mistaken belief that courage was a lack of fear. Courage is life's answer to fear.

When Dorothy misses the balloon ride home to Kansas, she thinks she's stuck in Oz forever, but Glinda, her wise inner guide, tells her she had what it took inside her all along to return home—in this case, home represents a fully integrated self that stands up to tough challenges, conquers fear, is able to conquer her inner critic, and reconnect with her love for her friends and family. Her true heart's desire was in her own backyard. By clicking her personal power together three times and repeating her mantra, "There's no place like home," she wakes up in her bed in Kansas, with all her friends and family by her side.

The Wizard of Oz illustrates everything you need to get to your act 3 resolve:

1. The identification of your core **challenge,** an **antagonist** to provide you with opportunities for growth, and the **courage** to go on a journey and begin writing **a new life script**

2. The willingness to work on yourself and **develop your character**

3. **Creativity** and **personal sovereignty**

4. The ability to hear guidance from your **wise inner director**

5. Acknowledgement that it is up to you to **take the lead in your life** and do what's required to overcome the challenge

6. The confidence to **speak your mind** and stand up to injustice

7. **Supporting players** to accompany you on your journey

8. A clear **vision**

9. Courage to **remove things from your life** that no longer serve you (fears, beliefs, judgments, antagonists) in order to find your true heart's desire

10. **Remaining unattached** to the outcome or *how* it will resolve in order to receive your act 3 resolution

The Wizard of Oz is the foundation film for this book. We will be revisiting this movie and all of its symbolism throughout.

Dorothy's Transformation

ACT 2

Mind
Believe she is smart
enough to find a solution

Courage
Confront Gulch.
Kill the witch.

Heart
Home is where the heart
is. Her true heart's desire
is in her own backyard.

ACT 1

ACT 3

Challenge:
Keep Toto.
Find her way home

Resolution:
Wakes up in Kansas.
Keeps Toto.

The Wonderful Wizard of Oz was the best-selling children's book of 1900. The author, L. Frank Baum, was the son-in-law of a suffragette and married to a champion of women's rights. In the first edition of the book, he wrote, "The old time fairy tale, having served for generations, may now be classed as 'historical' in the children's library; for the time has come for a series of newer 'wonder tales' in which the stereotyped genie, dwarf, and fairy are eliminated, together with all the horrible and blood-curdling incidents devised by their authors to point a fearsome moral to each tale. Modern education includes morality; therefore the modern child seeks only entertainment in its wonder tales and gladly dispenses with all disagreeable incident."

Baum may not have intended his story to teach morality, but symbolically, the story contains lessons in personal growth and transformation. By overcoming fear and self-doubt, developing a positive mindset, and acknowledging what's truly in your heart, you can achieve your vision. There's no need to go searching for your true heart's desire, it's right here, in your own backyard—in other words, within *you*.

The Wizard of Oz Symbolism

Cyclone	Vortex, catalyst for change
Emerald City	Love of self. Home is where the heart is. Integration of your body, mind, and spirit. No need to go looking for your own heart's desire, it's right within you. Green: Heart Chakra
Falling asleep in the poppy field	Desire to give up, go lie down, especially just before a breakthrough
Flying monkeys, hostile apple trees	Life's petty annoyances and roadblocks. Some people won't like you. So what.
Fork in the road	Every path offers an opportunity for growth.
Glinda, the Good Witch of the North	Inner film director, inner wisdom, intuition, wise guide. Supportive coach. "Find your true north."
Kill the witch	Conquer your fears.
Lion	Courage. Life's answer to fear. Self-confidence
Oz	Environment for growth.
Rainbow	Chakras, boundary between inner and outer world
Ruby Slippers	Personal power. Stay grounded. Know you have everything you need. Red: Root Chakra
Scarecrow	Mind. Self-esteem. Listen to the voice of your inner film director.

Scarecrow, Tin Man, and Lion	Surround yourself with supportive friends.
Surrender, Dorothy	Let go. Trust in the Divine (God, Universe, etc.)
There's no place like home	Thoughts shape reality. Affirmations / mantras work. True heart's desires can't be found "somewhere over the rainbow," but in our own back yards, in other words, within you.
Tin Man (Tin Woodsman)	Heart. Self-love. Love for others. Know you are lovable.
Toto	Love, protection
Wicked Witch of the East	Desire to have problems disappear in an instant.
Wicked Witch of the West	The antagonist—obstacle to forward movement. Opportunity to face fear. Outward manifestation of the inner film critic.
Wizard "just a man"	Desire to look to others for answers, especially from an oracle (prince, knight, wizard, fairy godmother)
Yellow Brick Road	Self-esteem, self-confidence. Trust yourself enough to follow the path, even though you can't see the entire road before you or how you'll get back "home." Go one step at a time. Yellow: Solar Plexus Chakra.

The Three-Act Structure of Film

Movies are written in three acts. The first act introduces us to the main character, otherwise known as the protagonist, hero, or heroine, and whatever conflict or challenge she (or he) faces. The goal of the screenwriter is to get her to the final act of the story having resolved the conflict or overcome the challenge in a way that inspires the audience.

In order to be a compelling story, the protagonist must experience a powerful transformation—a transition from the first act to the third that enables her to achieve her goal and come out in the end as a winner.

The best stories hold our attention throughout, because we are able to live vicariously through the main character. We can relate to her situation, even though it may be something completely foreign to our real lives. We may never know what it's like to own a farm in Africa, battle aliens on a space ship, survive the Titanic, or have schizophrenia, but we can relate to the character nonetheless. We may not know what it's like to be stuck in the land of Oz, but we all have felt stuck in one way or another. Because it isn't the specifics of the situation we connect with—it's the journey of the self that we all experience that makes us say *yes, I get it* and to desire more than anything for her to have a happy ending. We want to walk out of the theater feeling good.

A great movie allows us to completely lose ourselves in the story. We can forget our own lives for a couple of hours as we root for her success in the same way we'd want an audience to cheer us on if the story were about us.

The beauty of watching another person's story play out in film is that we have the advantage of being the objective observer. In many cases we can see through the character's words, actions, and body language what weaknesses, fears, beliefs, and assumptions she needs to let go of in order to resolve the problem she faces. The surprise is in discovering how she will do it, what predicaments she will be placed in, opportunities she'll be presented with, people she'll come across, and changes she will make in order to get to the finish line. Every scene presents a new opportunity for growth.

Our Lives in Three Acts

I've come to view our lives as flowing through three acts, just like a movie. In the grand scheme of things, our entire lives flow through childhood (act 1), adulthood (act 2), and old age (act 3). When you think about it, childhood and old age tend to be shorter than adulthood, the stage of life that lasts the longest, just like the second act of a movie. We also tend to spend a large chunk of our adulthood getting over the challenges of childhood in one way or another, and if we're lucky, we settle into our old age wiser for the experience.

Perhaps the meaning of life is to learn how to overcome personal challenges so that you can move on to the next phase of your existence, whatever that may be, having grown spiritually. In fact it's a theme in the movie reviewed in the first step, *Defending Your Life* by Albert Brooks, which is described in a scene included in your Star Pack called *I'm on Trial for Being Afraid?*

The challenges we face generally fall into one of three main areas: love, work, and self. Every one of us must deal with conflict, hardship, heartache, frustration, insecurity, and a whole host of other issues when it comes to ourselves, our work, and our interactions with people. The particulars may vary from person to person, but we all go through the human experience together. None of us are immune to adversity. Most of the time our problems are small and can be resolved in short order, or perhaps over a period of time. We set business goals, check items off a daily list of chores, or tend to the minutiae of our everyday lives with relative ease.

But when the issue is big—when the challenge we face isn't an easy one—that's where we can get tripped up. That's when we can get stuck.

Take weight loss, for example. Let's say you're watching a movie, and in the first act you are introduced to a character as she stares at her reflection in a full-length mirror with a look of despair on her face. She struggles to squeeze into her jeans. She lies down on the bed to button them and covers herself up with a bulky sweater to hide her muffin top. When she opens her kitchen cabinets, there is a bottle of weight-loss pills sitting beside a bag of potato chips.

Through observing her morning routine, you know she's unhappily overweight, and it's getting serious, because her clothes don't fit. She loves junk food, but instead of giving it up, she takes a pill. Even though many of us know what it's like to be overweight, love food, and wish there was a magic pill that would cause us to become thinner without making any lifestyle changes, you can see through observation, and you know intuitively, that the pills won't work. She needs to give up the chips.

On the reality TV show, *The Biggest Loser*, the first act of the series begins with a group of overweight people who have decided to enter into a competition to see who can lose the most weight. The goal is to make it to the final act of the show as the "biggest loser" and take home the grand prize. Act 2 is the difficult process they endure where they must eat well, exercise like mad, and deal with the emotional and mental blocks that have kept them fat.

Act 2 is the hard part, and that's why many of us stay stuck in act 1. Who wants to eat right and exercise more? That's no fun. Not to mention the cravings, temptations, and other obstacles that get in the way of our progress. No wonder weight loss is a billion-dollar industry. Every program promises the same thing: an easy way to get to your act 3 resolve.

And that's the problem. We want to jump straight from act 1 to act 3 when we're faced with the big challenges of life. We look for the magic pill, foolproof system, get-rich-quick scheme, and promise of overnight success. We hope things will change so we won't have to. We wait for the prince, fairy, genie, or fairy godmother to come so she will wave her magic wand or sprinkle a little fairy dust over us and transform our lives *for us*. We don't want to have to go through our act 2, because it's scary and hard, it requires sacrifice, a total shift in thinking, a change in behavior, and that we give up certain beliefs and face reality head-on. It also takes time. It requires that we go one step at a time. Not knowing the exact outcome is disconcerting. Fear and doubt creep in. Just the thought of it makes us want to go lie down and put it off another day. Most people do, until something comes along that makes staying where we are—stuck in act 1—more uncomfortable than going through the changes required of act 2.

A woman receives a cancer diagnosis and can no longer justify her pack-a-day smoking habit. A man receives a pink slip at work. A woman is given a poor job evaluation. A man's wife is arrested for drunk and disorderly conduct and can no longer ignore the fact that their child is in being endangered. A woman's husband is caught cheating with his co-worker.

For years, she knew smoking was bad for her health, but she didn't quit. He knew his company was going to be laying people off a year ago, but he never looked for a job. She sensed her boss didn't trust her abilities, yet she still didn't share positive client feedback with him, rationalizing that she was being humble. He knew his wife was an alcoholic, but he kept hoping she'd stop drinking. She knew her husband had lost interest in her, but she didn't want to face the changes she'd need to make if they divorced.

Why do we do these things? Why do we procrastinate, live in denial, and settle for the status quo? What is it that makes us stay stuck in bad situations?

The same is true for positive challenges. How many people say they want to write a book someday but never do it, wish they had a college degree but never get one, long to own their own home but never buy one, collect travel brochures but never go anywhere, and otherwise don't go after their dreams?

Life would be easy if getting through act 2 didn't require anything of us. If change were easy, we'd know what to do and how to do it, and there would be no physical, mental, or emotional pieces to the equation we couldn't solve with ease. It's human nature to want things to work out on their own. Sometimes they do. Often they don't.

Something I've learned and come to accept is that you can't do something until you're ready. You can't leave a bad relationship until you're ready. You can't leave a job to pursue something else until you're ready. You can't make changes in your health and fitness until you're ready. You can't enter into a new relationship until you're ready. Readiness can't be forced. Think of all the times when you wished a friend would make a move—when you could see they were making a mistake, but they wouldn't listen. Everyone could see they were going down a rabbit hole, but they needed to figure things out for themselves, just as you do. Life is a transformative process. Like any good film, you need to get through act 2 to get to your act 3 resolve, but something needs to shift inside you before you can take the first step. At some point, you'll find yourself holding your own version of a twenty dollar car scraper, and everything will begin to shift.

The area where you feel stuck—whether it's something to do with yourself, your relationships, or your career, will feel like an opposing magnet. It'll be all you can do to enter the front doors to the building where you work if you are ready to leave. Telling your partner it's over will almost feel like a voice coming through you, not from you. The alcohol, cigarettes, and junk food will be in the trash. Everything in you will tell you it's time.

This book is designed to help walk you through this transformative journey through *your* act 2 if you are ready, and if you're not, to help set the stage for the time when you will be.

Life, just like a movie, is a process that flows through three acts. Whenever your life takes an unexpected turn, you feel trapped, you're experiencing self-doubt, you're looking for some direction, you're faced with a personal challenge, you have a dream, or you'd like to be reminded of your personal truth, come back to this, your personal guidebook through the three acts of your life story, and remember that *you* are the star. Nothing and no one can take away your personal power unless you let it happen.

Like Dorothy and all of the other movie heroes and heroines in this book, you have what it takes to get through your second act and resolve any challenge. It all starts with a choice to lead your life with the courage to begin writing a new life script based on your own definition of happiness and success. When you reach *that* final act, the real show begins.

STEP ONE

Embrace Your Inner Screenwriter

Lead with Courage

Defending Your Life

Int. Daniel Miller's Home.
Daniel and his wife are sitting across the table
from one another.

> DANIEL
> Do this for me. It helps.

> DANIEL'S WIFE
> Not now. I'm eating.

> DANIEL
> Come on, do it.

> DANIEL'S WIFE
> What do you want me to do?

> DANIEL
> Be him.

> DANIEL'S WIFE
> This is silly.

> DANIEL
> It's not silly. It helps me. Offer
> me fifty-five thousand, no more.

> DANIEL'S WIFE
> How much do you want?

> DANIEL
> How much you offering me?

> DANIEL'S WIFE
> Fifty-five thousand dollars.

> DANIEL
> I can't work here for a penny
> under sixty-five, I'm sorry.

> DANIEL'S WIFE
> Well I can't pay you sixty-five.

> DANIEL
> Then I can't work here.

                    DANIEL'S WIFE
               Fifty-eight thousand.

                       DANIEL
                    Sixty-five.

                    DANIEL'S WIFE
                    Fifty-nine.

                       DANIEL
                    Sixty-five.

                    DANIEL'S WIFE
                      Sixty?

                       DANIEL
                    Sixty-five.

                    DANIEL'S WIFE
                    Sixty-one.

                       DANIEL
          Let me make it plain. I cannot take the job
          for under sixty-five, under no conditions.

Cut to: Int. Courtroom, Judgment City

                    LENA FOSTER
Your honors, I would like to go directly to the
next afternoon and show you the real encounter.

A scene from Daniel's life appears on the screen.
He is sitting across from the interviewer's desk.

                    INTERVIEWER
          Daniel, I'm prepared to offer you
             forty-nine thousand dollars.
                       DANIEL
                    I'll take it.

                    INTERVIEWER
          (taken aback)Let me get you a parking place.
                       DANIEL
                      Okay.

Defending Your Life

On the 1991 comedy, *Defending Your Life*, Daniel Miller (Albert Brooks) takes his new car out for a spin and winds up getting killed in an accident with a bus. He ends up in the afterlife at a place called Judgment City.

Judgment city is the place people go after they die where they must demonstrate how they displayed courage on earth and overcame their fears. If they can prove that, they get to move to the next level. If not, they must go back to earth to try again. Daniel is reassured that he's not on trial, although he has an attorney, a prosecutor, and two judges. They show scenes from his life where he allowed himself to be bullied on the playground. He chickened out of giving a speech that would have had a positive impact on his career. He bought a car that was less than what he wanted. And in the scene you read at the beginning of this chapter, he was afraid to negotiate his salary.

While Daniel is in Judgment City, he meets and falls in love with Julia (Meryl Streep). Julia lived an exemplary life and is put up at the Majestic, a posh hotel that's much better than the Holiday Inn-type place where Daniel is staying. She showed courage in her life and impressed the judges so much that they ask to view—several times—the scene where she rescued her children from a house fire. Even in the Past-lives Pavilion, she shows up as Prince Valiant, while Daniel is a native running from a wild beast.

Daniel is ultimately sentenced to another life on earth, because he is still allowing his fears to rule his life—or in this case, his afterlife. At the trial, the prosecuting attorney (Lee Grant) shows a scene from the night before. Even though Daniel is attracted to Julia, he turned down her invitation to spend the night. He wanted to, but he was too afraid of screwing something up.

Daniel's antagonist is the prosecuting attorney, Lena Foster, who shows how Daniel repeatedly missed out on opportunities, backed away in fear, and failed to act courageously.

Daniel's antagonist *literally* points out his inability to face his fears. The objects of Daniel's fear, Lena Foster and the judges, are there to teach him how to be courageous. Brooks does a brilliant job of creating a story that mirrors real life.

In act 3, Daniel is sitting on the bus, resigned to his fate, waiting to be taken to his next earthly life, symbolic of how he is still stuck in "act 1" of his existence because he hasn't had the courage to move forward. When he sees Julia on her bus, headed for the next level, he finally faces his fears and takes a leap of faith. He jumps off his bus to join Julia on hers. The judges see this act of courage and allow him to move on to the next level. Interestingly, his earthly life ends with a bus, and his next life begins on a bus.

The metaphor of "You're either on the bus or off the bus" came from the Merry Pranksters. Known for going on acid trips, the group traveled across the country in 1964 in a colorfully painted bus. "You are either *attuned* to the group consciousness or you are *not* attuned to the group consciousness." (Not sure this is what the Brooks intended, but you never know!) Choosing faith and courage over fear and inaction is to raise your level of consciousness.

The Role of the Screenwriter

Screenwriting is, at root, a collaborative form of writing.

A screenplay is primarily two things: a blueprint for a movie and a business plan. The job of the screenwriter is to tell a certain kind of story as crisply and efficiently as possible, in an effort to get others enthused about forming a team and raising a production budget to make a movie.

A writer can get fired from the team developing his own script, and such firings are not unusual. Producers, directors, and primary actors all outrank screenwriters and can suggest script changes.

(Charles Deemer http://www.filmunderground.com/134/Article/NWFS/The-Role-of-the-Screenwriter.htm)

Embrace Your Inner Screenwriter
Lead with Courage

What if you discovered that your life was a movie and, what's more, this entire time you've been its scriptwriter? Have you been creating drama, comedy, action-adventure, or tragedy? Most likely it's been a combination of these themes.

Think about an area of your life that you'd like to change. Is it possible that, in your mind, you've treated the situation like melodrama—or worse, a horror movie?

Memorable movies begin with a great script. The screenwriter creates the characters—who they are—and who lives in their world, loves them, tests them, causes them pain or difficulty—what they look like, what interests them, and how they behave. The writer also creates each scene, describes the situation, sets up the conflict, and allows us to play voyeur to the protagonist's hopes, struggles, and solutions. The writer brings us through each act, maintaining our interest as we wait to find out what she'll do, how she'll change, and how it will all resolve in the end. The story comes through the writer. What she writes is what manifests itself on the screen.

In your life movie, however, there will be changes, because unlike a real movie, not all of the circumstances of life are within your control. There are events that are bigger than one person—recession, death, divorce, and layoffs, for example. Furthermore, in real life, your costars are writing *their* own scripts, too. They may not want to follow your script at all, just as you may not feel obligated to follow theirs. Not only that, but your director (inner wisdom) may point you in new directions that you never would have considered before. Circumstances can change, which can influence the storyline. Just like the real-life role of a movie screenwriter, other people will influence what you create. If your life were perfect, you'd be quite boring from an audience's perspective. All interesting stories, even fairy tales, are based on conflict. It's the journey of overcoming that conflict that makes a great film.

Throughout our lives we are faced with challenges, and we often get stuck, because we don't want to do what may be required to get unstuck. Much of that has to do with fear. The script we write for ourselves is based on our fears, instead of faith.

I'm sure you've heard fear defined as "False Evidence Appearing Real." In other words, we may have nothing to fear (except fear itself, as Franklin Delano Roosevelt once said), but we imagine our situation as far worse than it is. We treat it like a Stephen King movie.

Think of the movie *Cujo* for a moment. A mother and her young son go to see a mechanic (who lives out in the middle of nowhere) to have her car fixed. When they arrive, a rabid dog, Cujo, is outside, waiting to attack. Her car is now completely broken down, it's hotter than hell outside, and the car becomes an oven. The majority of this movie's second act is spent watching her try to find a way to escape, while her son is slowly dying of thirst. Her husband doesn't come looking for her for days, because he'd just found out she'd been sleeping with her tennis coach.

Her act 3 resolution comes when the situation inside the car becomes more frightening than the situation outside. In spite of the dog, she takes her child and makes a run for the house, because it's her only hope to revive him. A gun sits on the kitchen table. She's able to grab it just as Cujo comes crashing through the kitchen window. Her husband shows up shortly thereafter, and presumably, because of what she's been through, they live happily ever after.

Think of this movie as a metaphor. Have you ever found yourself in a bad situation, but you were so afraid to change that you waited until it got really bad before you did something about it? Or maybe it wasn't so bad; it just wasn't so good—wasn't what you wanted. Chances are, there is no rabid dog or other type of beast waiting for you "out there," but you've made it out to be something like that in your imagination. Like Daniel Miller, your fears may have held such a grip on you that you settled for less, and as a result, you were sentenced to repeating the life lesson, or in his case, the life.

Time to write a new script!

But just as the definition at the beginning of this chapter suggests, you won't have full control. Producers, directors, and actors will have input. Keep one rule in mind from here on out. You may love the idea of writing a new script in which your bad boss, irritating spouse, or wicked witch in your story suddenly becomes the person you want them to be. Unfortunately, they will remain true to character. The only character in your life story that you ever have the power to change is your own.

First Chakra: Root

The first chakra, or root chakra, is located at the base of your spine and pertains to your feet, knees, legs, lower spine, mouth, teeth, intestines, and bones—the structure of the body. It is your survival chakra. Its element is earth, and its color is red. It is your foundation. Someone with a healthy, balanced first chakra feels safe in the world and has a sense of prosperity. Someone who is deficient in root chakra energy may be anorexic, as though they don't want to take up

*"Fool, that
I am! I should have
remembered—those
slippers will never
come off, as long as
you're alive."*

*—Wicked Witch
of the West*

space. Someone with an excess of root chakra energy may be overweight, as if they are constantly trying to ground themselves. While weight issues may indicate an imbalance in the first chakra, a first chakra imbalance can manifest itself in other ways as well. People with a root chakra imbalance may fear change and become attached to what *is*. The element of the first chakra is earth, and its demon is *fear*.

As we saw in the scene from *Defending Your Life* at the start of this chapter, Daniel is faced with negotiating his salary, but when it comes time to do it in real life, he is so gripped by fear that he accepts his new employer's first offer. A major theme of *Defending Your Life* is the idea that you cannot move forward in life, or in the evolution of your spirit, until you've learned to overcome unrealistic fears. What's the worst that could have happened to Daniel if he had asked for sixty-five thousand dollars or had to do a bit of haggling to arrive at a decent salary? In his mind he would have lost the job. He'd already scripted a scene in his head in which the hiring manager grew red in the face and told him to get the bleep out of his office; Daniel would have lost his chance to work for that company. In reality, hiring managers fully expect a person to push back on their first offer. Daniel may not have gotten sixty-five, but I bet he would have gotten a lot more than forty-nine, and either way, he would have walked away from the meeting feeling a heck of a lot better about himself. Check out the *Defending Your Life* Negotiation Scene in your Star Pack. You'll see by the look on Daniel's face exactly how he felt when he accepted the first offer. You may think that an employer would be happy to get cheap help, but I bet Daniel wouldn't be on the top of his boss's list for promotion, being such a pushover. Judging by the look on his face, Daniel totally lost his respect.

I personally find negotiating to be incredibly uncomfortable, but instead of shrinking away from it, I see it as an opportunity to confront my fears and hone my abilities in this area. One of the reasons why men tend to out-earn women is because men (aside from Daniel) aren't afraid to negotiate. Women often fail to know their own worth, and even know just how incredible they are and how valuable their work is to the people they serve.

When I was offered a job, I pushed back on their salary and bonus offer. I paced the hallway outside of a class I was taking while I spoke to my future employer on my cell phone. I was nervous as all get-out, but I did it anyway, and I got what I asked for. I really wanted the position, but I wouldn't have felt good about it had I accepted their initial offer, which would have been a lousy way to start that new job. I would have felt undervalued by my employer—because I had undervalued myself (and isn't that what we are *really* mad about when we settle for less?) Resentment isn't a good emotion to take to work with you.

When I was promoted to a management position, I pushed back on their initial offer again, in spite of my fear, and wound up getting *over three times* the salary increase they first offered.

As a speaker, I have to negotiate with event planners. That old fear—that I will lose the opportunity—is still there, but as I once heard someone say, if you never say no, your yeses don't mean anything. If you want to be valued as an employee or a business owner, (or as a wife, girlfriend, partner, friend) you must value yourself. What have you got to lose? The key is in how you say it, which you'll learn about in step six: *Learn Your Lines.*

My son once told me he was afraid to call a place where he'd submitted a job application. I told him that's what courage was for, and this seemed to resonate with him. Fear and anxiety hit our survival center. The stress kicks in a natural fight or flight response. Think of Dorothy again—her first reaction to fear is to run away. Her inner cowardly lion's first reaction is to fight. "Put 'em up...put 'em up. I'll fight you with two hands tied behind my back. I'll fight you with my eyes closed."

I've found dozens of on-line surveys listing common fears. They include flying, heights, pain, disappointment, commitment, fear of the unknown, loneliness, ridicule, rejection, death, failure, public speaking, and a big one—humiliation. Here's an interesting web page that lists phobias in alphabetical order: http://www.angelsghosts.com/state_of_fear.html. Did you know that scriptophobia is the fear of writing in public? I didn't know there was such a thing, but I think I have it. I'm more of a private writer.

It seems to me that the only thing you can really do is know what you want, create a plan and work it, and have faith that everything will turn out as it's supposed to.

Far too often, when people talk about overcoming fear, they talk about it in terms of going after something big. And for whatever reason, skydiving seems to be the activity of choice that's supposed to help you overcome whatever holds you back. Jumping out of an airplane is somehow supposed to help you conquer other big fears, usually something to do with your profession. Walking on hot coals comes in a closes second, followed by bungee jumping or breaking a board with your bare hands. I have no desire to do any of these things. I'm beginning to think it takes more courage to live a simple life. To say you don't aspire to be CEO, celebrity, or multi-millionaire takes courage in a society that has increasingly become more materialistic and infatuated with fame and fortune. Even regular people are becoming rich and famous for exposing their lives on reality television. Success has been defined with such high expectations that few people can meet, it's no wonder antidepressants are the third most commonly prescribed drug in America and antianxiety medication ranks in the top ten.

It's why I love yoga so much. It gets me out of my head and into the here and now. Imagine for a moment that you're digging your hands into some fresh garden soil. You're not up in your head, but connected to the earth. Instead of feeling anxious, you're connected to the present moment and secure in your place in the world. Breathe slowly and deeply. As you inhale, think of bringing more peace to your body and mind. As you exhale, think of letting go of stress and tension.

To be grounded is to be in your body. Your body houses your spirit. It is the first structural form you embrace. People need structure in their lives. The products of our creativity come about when we give them a place to live. Here are some examples:

- The foundation and framework of a house.
- Fourteen lines of a sonnet.
- Three acts of a movie or play.
- Intro, verses, and choruses of a song.
- Chapters and section headers of a book.
- Introduction, three main points, and conclusion of a speech.

Even a daily list of things to do can help provide structure to your day and keep you focused. Life itself is structure. It's a place for your spirit to learn and grow (or at least I like to think of it that way). Healthy marriages can form a structure upon which to build a wonderful life. At times, you may resist structure, but when you embrace it, it actually helps you to create. The free spirit in me resents being told what to do, but as liberated as I like to be, I could never have finished this book if I hadn't first laid its framework. If you take a moment to flip through its pages, you'll see that it follows a set pattern. Once I had it in place, all I had to do was fill in each section. Giving your life and your creative projects a framework is grounding, meaning, it helps you feel more at peace and less scattered.

I've suffered many injuries to my feet over the years, and while a lot of those injuries can be attributed to activity, I've also come to notice that my feet tend to act up when I'm not listening to my body. When I'm not moving in the right direction—or not moving at all—in some area of my life, or when I'm not paying attention to my intuition, my feet speak to me, as strange as that may sound. Back when I first began my yoga practice, I could say that I was trapped in a bad marriage, but what I was really stuck in was a state of confusion over who I was and what I wanted for my life. I didn't want to believe what my intuition was telling me, either. I was unable to make a decision about how best to proceed. My boys came first. When I was able to make peace with my life as it was in the present moment, and through letting things go energetically through my yoga practice, my foot pain subsided. My feet still act up from time to time, and when they do, I always stop and ask myself what I'm afraid of. (And sometimes I just take an Advil.)

For you it could be a weight issue or something else pertaining to the first chakra. The messages say *pay attention, make changes, get unstuck, and notice when you're playing to your fears instead of moving forward with faith that your intuition is guiding you appropriately.*

We all know that obesity is a problem in America. Based on diet alone, I'm not surprised. The *Frontline* documentary, "Poor Kids," showed the impacts of poverty on American children from a child's viewpoint. One little girl described how food was so scarce in her household that her family often resorted to eating frozen pizzas because they were cheaper than whole foods, which is why she was overweight. According to the United States Department of Agriculture (USDA), 16.7 million children under eighteen in the United States live in households where they are unable to consistently access enough nutritious food necessary for a healthy life.

According to a survey conducted by CareerBuilder, Inc., 44 percent of respondents gained weight as a result of their jobs. People are working longer hours for less pay, and fear speaking out or leaving because their livelihood is at stake. These are just two examples of how fear for survival—and literal survival in terms of scarcity of food—affects your first chakra.

In *The Wizard of Oz*, Dorothy's personal power, which symbolically allowed her to stand up to her antagonist, the Wicked Witch of the West, was contained in her ruby slippers—ruby/red, the color of the first chakra. The witch was constantly trying to steal her shoes (or take her power away) and scare her into submission. The antagonist of a story is really just an outward manifestation of something that needs to be dealt with inside the mind, heart, and spirit of the protagonist. Lena Foster is there to show Daniel Miller how he's allowing his fears to stall his spiritual development. The witch is an outward manifestation of Dorothy's fear that she is powerless in the face of Gulch, who embodies her fear that her life is not within her control. In Oz, she is grounded in her root chakra, her survival energy. She stays tight inside those shoes and accesses her courage (her cowardly lion) to walk the yellow brick road, follow her path with faith, and stand up to fear.

To embrace your inner screenwriter is to acknowledge that while you don't have full control over the things that happen in your life, you do have the power to write your story in a way that honors faith over fear. Stay grounded in your first chakra energy and trust that life will support you and your inner wisdom will guide you. Acknowledge your act 1 challenge and begin to visualize what you want your act 3 resolution to look like. By doing so, you can move into your act 2, stand up to your fears, and connect with whatever it is you need so that you can reach where you want to go.

In the first act of *Defending Your Life*, Daniel tries to prove to the judges that he is worthy of moving on to the next stage of his spiritual development instead of returning to earth. He finally accomplishes this when he gets in touch with what's in his heart: he loves Julia. He chooses faith over fears, and takes a literal leap of faith when he jumps off his bus and onto hers.

The script he'd written and followed his whole life—or in this case, *lives*—was dictated by the demon of the first chakra (as though life were some sort of horror movie not to be trusted). He finally chooses to write a new one, based on faith. And what gets him moving? His feet. Daniel realizes that he's on the wrong bus, yet again, headed in the wrong direction. He finally decides that he doesn't have to go where other people told him he had to go. He decides what's right for him, takes a risk, and leaps off the old bus (fear) and onto the new one (courage).

Daniel's Transformation

ACT 2

Mind
Chooses faith over fear

Heart
Loves Julia

Courage
Leaps off bus

ACT 1

ACT 3

Challenge:
Prove to judges fear
doesn't rule his life

Resolution:
Moves
To next Stage

Summary

What role does courage play in your life right how? Stepping into your act 2 and taking on the challenge you're dealing with requires courage—not only in the face of fear, but in the face of what's required of you—the work involved. You may think it's easier to stay put and do nothing—to never change your own outlook or behavior. But that's just it, where you are is painful in its own way. You have to face the pain of change in order to move past it, or stay where you are with no end in sight.

Identify the core essence of who you are, examine the stories you've been telling yourself, and choose to write a new and better script for your life, one step at a time.

Real Courage

My great uncle, Johnny Anderson, was twenty-nine years old in 1942 when he enlisted in the United States Army. He became a Ranger, and after he finished his training, he was sent to Northern Africa to fight the Germans. He was in two major battles. During the second invasion of Sicily, on August 10, 1943, he sustained multiple gunshot wounds to his legs, arms, and chest, and was left bleeding in the battlefield, surrounded by the bodies of dead and wounded soldiers. Approximately ten hours later, a Jehova Witness, wearing a simple white robe and a cross around his neck, walked through the field in search of men who were still breathing. Johnny was one of those men.

He was treated at a front-line hospital and given two quarts of blood before he was flown to another hospital in Northern Africa. A doctor wanted to amputate one of his legs, but another doctor insisted that it could be saved and sent him back to the States where he would spend the next two years at Ashford General Hospital in West Virginia. He underwent multiple surgeries and slowly recovered from his injuries. As my grandmother, Johnny's sister, described it, they "stiffened" his leg, rather than amputate it. For the rest of his life, my uncle walked around as if that leg were tied to a board. But that never stopped him from walking all over town to his wallpapering and painting jobs—work he'd started when he was only twelve-years-old.

Johnny marched and fought during WWII for a year before he was injured in battle. When he was oversees, he would occasionally write home, and in one of the letters to his younger brother, Freddie, he wrote, "All I want to do is go home and stand in the brook."

A brook ran through my great-grandparent's back yard, not too far from the house. Their home was situated on a fairly busy street that led to the center of town, and it sat on the right side of the property—the left side yard being bigger than the back.

When Johnny returned from the war, he did just what he said he wanted to do. He stood in that brook. And over time, as he stood there, comforted by the serenity of the water that flowed from the hills and down into the valley, bubbling up over rocks and bringing with it some trout and a turtle or two, he began to build. First, a foot bridge that extended from one side of the brook to the other, and then a water wheel, painted a gorgeous, deep red. Rhododendrons sat against the hill on the other side, and flowers were planted along the edges. Over time, Johnny and his father, a stonemason, built a lily pad pond, and he would stock it each summer with goldfish that were bigger than any I'd ever seen. We loved trying to catch the bullfrogs that would sit on the lily pads in the summertime, but they'd hop away as soon as we came too close. It's when I learned that goldfish grew to the size of their tanks, and I figured they must have been pretty bummed out when winter came and they had to either fit in the smaller tank my uncle kept in his basement, or in the one embedded in the wall of the sun room that entertained us when we were kids.

Over time, the yard was fully landscaped with carefully edged flowerbeds full of begonias, impatiens, petunias, and a wide variety of annuals. There were statues and water fountains surrounded by lush green grass. A sun dial that sat atop a three-foot-tall stone pillar told the time of day. I used to love sitting with my cousins on a white, wrought-iron love seat and pretend we lived in another era.

In the far left corner was a pigeon coop that housed a variety of the birds. One of them, whom Johnny called Tony, would often come sit on his shoulder as he mowed the grass or watered the flowers.

One day Johnny was inside, listening to classical music, when there was a knock on the door. He got up to find a young couple standing on his front steps.

"Mr. Anderson?" said the young woman. She was half giggling as she spoke, full of hope and excitement. She introduced herself and her fiancé. "We're getting married on Sunday. We were wondering, Mr. Anderson—well, we drive by your house almost every day and we so admire your gardens. And we were wondering, if you wouldn't mind, would be all right if we had our wedding pictures taken in your yard?"

Johnny smiled and said, "Of course you can. I'd be honored to have you here on your big day."

Word quickly spread throughout town that Johnny Anderson's yard on Margaret Street in Monson, Massachusetts, was the place to have your wedding photos and prom pictures taken. It was the place to have portraits done and to exchange your wedding vows. Weekends got to be so busy that Johnny had to keep a calendar to stay organized and to ensure that everyone had their fair share of time. He could often be seen on his screened-in porch, sitting in a rocker with his leg up. He'd smoke unfiltered Camels and watch as couples got married and teenagers smiled awkwardly in their tuxedos and gowns.

When Johnny returned home from the war, he stood in the brook and beautified its surroundings to the point that the yard became an oasis, and people started to come. Every weekend during the warmer months, my uncle's yard became the perfect backdrop to the community's most cherished photographs, and he never accepted a dime for the privilege. It was his pleasure.

Occasionally, people would leave a donation in an envelope and slip it in his mailbox, knowing he'd never accept it in person, but Johnny would just pass the money along to one of the local churches. Even though he was a member of the Congregational Church and on the board of directors for years, he didn't discriminate when it came to the money people gave him. He didn't do it for the money.

As a young man, Johnny Anderson was a soldier who faced one of the most challenging experiences of life—war. He marched to the brink of exhaustion, battled Nazi soldiers, witnessed the death of many friends, and endured unimaginable pain in a hospital far from home, all the while picturing himself standing in the brook back home.

That brook and the gardens he built around it became a field of dreams that attracted people from all over who wanted to capture their lives' most precious moments. It kept a smile on Johnny's face, an open door to his heart, and no signs of shell-shock, right up until about two years before his death at age eighty-eight.

When he was in his late seventies, Johnny switched to filtered Camels, and not too long after that, he stopped smoking entirely. He said, "I just decided they weren't good for me anymore." Soon he had to spend time throughout the day hooked up to an oxygen tank to help him breathe. He didn't come out and say it, but we suspected emphysema. Whatever it was, we knew his doctor couldn't operate—there was too much shrapnel in his chest.

As his body grew weaker from illness, he needed to bring in the help of landscapers. That worked for a while. Johnny would grab his cane and do his best to work the grounds, but it came to a point where he couldn't work at all and he had to spend most of his time in bed. That's when the memories came flooding back.

Over the years, Johnny's friends would frequently join him on the porch to share a smoke and to talk. I'd always assumed there were war stories—talk he'd save for the men. It turned out I was wrong. Johnny hadn't talked about the war at all, until he could no longer keep the thoughts away.

"You never forget the smell," he said.

I used to visit Johnny and Esther, his sister and my great aunt. Neither Aunt Esther nor Uncle Johnny had ever married and stayed together in the family home. It had been about thirty years since my great-grandparents had passed way. We were all sitting around the kitchen table one day, talking, when Johnny started to shake all over. He put his hand to his forehead, as if to try to shove the memories back inside, and then he cried. My mother told me his psychiatrist recommended he talk about it. I didn't know what to say—I wanted to respect his privacy while at the same time let him know he could tell me whatever he wanted to. I stood up and put my hand on his shoulder.

"The smell of what?" I asked.

"Dead bodies," he said.

"We were marching for days," he continued. "The general said we were going to get the day off. But the men they sent to relieve us were shot down out of the sky—friendly fire."

He paused to catch his breath, then said, "And dead bodies don't come down any faster than live ones."

We sat in silence.

My uncle shook as he wept. "They expected too much," he said.

Johnny was afraid he wouldn't go to heaven because he'd killed people. The German soldiers were just kids—men like him, with families who cared about them. Even though memories of the war haunted him for the last couple years of his life, he said he lived a good life. He died at Wing Memorial Hospital on February 20, 2001.

Many soldiers carried pictures of their wives and girlfriends in their pockets; my uncle carried a picture in his mind of the brook that ran through his family's back yard and the gardens he'd grow around it when he returned home. He instinctively knew that the antidote to the intense fear he felt was to ground himself in the earth. Instead of reliving the fear of war when he returned home, he planted himself in the here and now by *literally* planting things. And in spite of his injuries, he moved. He didn't let his experience hold him back. He found his feet, and he walked—to his wallpapering and painting jobs, to his job as a clerk at the hardware store downtown, and around his yard.

I think we can all learn a lot from Johnny Anderson. When we find ourselves feeling fear and anxiety, we can ground ourselves in the here and now. Reconnecting to the earth, our center, the present moment, can calm us in the truth that we have everything we need to survive. The earth will support us. That's how it was designed.

Unfortunately, we have become so disconnected from that truth. Most of us buy all of our food at the supermarket, depend on an organization to provide us with work, look to our significant others to give us that feeling of safety and security, and look to sources outside of ourselves for what we need or to make us feel valuable. I didn't quite understand what it was about my uncle that I admired so much when I was a child, but now, I think it was his upbeat attitude and positive outlook. He believed that no matter what, everything will be as it's supposed to be. He didn't wait for life to be perfect before he chose to be happy.

My uncle didn't write a script for his life that involved reliving the pain of war. He didn't focus on his physical injuries, or on his psychic ones. Instead he wrote a new, more empowering script for his life that involved beauty and community and connection. He lived to be eighty-eight years old in spite of the fact that he smoked unfiltered Camel cigarettes for seventy years. I believe my uncle chose not to let the war define him as a victim. He could have wallowed in the misery of his experience, but instead, he chose to write an inspiring life story. Instead of living up in his head, haunted by the pain of war, he rooted himself deeply in the earth, literally, and grounded himself in the present, instead of in the past. He surrounded himself with the opposite of war— beauty, flowers, flowing water, and nature. He had something he was passionate about. His job paid the bills. The money he earned through his work put food on the table, but his passion fed his soul. My uncle got through the horror of war by holding tight to a vision of standing in a brook, and then continued with that vision when he returned by creating a magnificent landscape around it. He never married, but he loved everyone. It wasn't until he could no longer stand in the brook and tend to his gardens that his fears came flooding back, illustrating just how important it was to him, and to all of us, that we find a way to ground ourselves, to stay connected to the earth, and actively write our life stories to be a romantic adventure instead of a horror show.

Notes

Notes

STEP TWO

Develop Your Character

Lead with Light

Mirror Mirror

Int. The Seven Dwarves' cabin.
Snow White is standing, holding a sword.
The Prince and the dwarves are seated around a
table.

SNOW WHITE
Gentlemen, I can think of no greater warriors
to lead into battle…but this is my fight.

Snow White runs out of the cabin and locks the
door behind her. The prince runs to the door
to try to convince her to open it. They speak
through the barred window.

PRINCE
Open the door.

SNOW WHITE
You know, all that time locked up in the castle,
I did a lot of reading. I read so many stories
where the prince saves the princess in the end.

PRINCE
Open the door. Open the door, Snow.

SNOW WHITE
I think it's time we changed that ending.

Mirror Mirror

In *Mirror Mirror*, a comedy that came out in 2012, Snow White (Lilly Collins) lives with her evil stepmother, the wicked queen (Julia Roberts). The Queen is a cougar, determined to get the much-younger prince to marry her, but the prince has his eyes set on Snow White. As in the classic fairy tale, the queen orders the huntsman (Nathan Lane) to lure Snow White into the woods and return with her heart.

Snow White hides out with the seven dwarves. Instead of miners, the dwarves are thieves, but the princess charms them into changing their ways. The dwarves teach her how to fight, so instead of being a weak and passive princess, Snow White learns to be a warrior. Meanwhile, the queen has tricked the prince into drinking a love potion, which turns out to be for dogs—puppy love. He's now completely enamored with the Queen.

In a clever twist on the classic story, it's Snow White's kiss that releases the prince from the queen's spell. As you read in the opening script, she locks him inside the dwarves' cabin. Snow White decides to write a new script where it's she who storms the castle, beats the queen, saves her father, and finally marries the prince. In the final scene, an old and ugly queen arrives at her wedding with the poison apple, but Snow White doesn't take the bait, or in this case, the bite. Instead, she repeats back to the queen what she said to Snow White in act 1: "It's always good to know when you've been beaten."

Snow White and the Huntsman

Snow White and the Huntsman is the dramatic version of this classic fairy tale. Like a vampire, the queen (Charlize Theron), in order to stay alive and youthful, must suck the youth and beauty out of the young women in the kingdom. She locks Snow White (Kristen Stewart) in a castle cell after murdering Snow White's father, the king. When Snow White has grown into a beautiful young woman, the queen orders her brother to retrieve her. She wants Snow White's heart because draining her life force will feed her own. Snow White seizes the opportunity to escape by stabbing him with a nail she loosened from the castle walls.

Instead of treating Snow White as a weak and helpless victim, the huntsman, who is sent by the Queen to kill her, turns out to be a true knight—chivalrous, honorable, and empowering. He teaches her how to defend herself. Snow White may be a princess, but she is no damsel.

Snow White hides out with the seven dwarves, who are living in the forest in a land that has been deadened by the Queen's evil nature. The queen appears to Snow White as the prince, Snow White's childhood friend, instead of appearing as an old woman like the Disney classic. She gives Snow White the poison apple that induces her coma. But it's the huntsman's kiss, not the prince's, which breaks the spell. Snow White becomes a warrior princess, much like a Joan of Arc, and leads an entire army to storm the castle. In the end, she kills the wicked queen, saves everyone in the kingdom, and becomes their benevolent leader.

Pretty Woman

In this 1990 film, Edward (Richard Gere), a wealthy businessman who makes deals that are legal but destructive, hires Vivian (Julia Roberts), a Hollywood prostitute, to be his escort. Throughout the story, they try to maintain a shallow relationship based solely on sex, but wind up getting to know one another and falling in love. Edward is in the process of making a business deal that would be very lucrative for his firm but would put a man, who has spent his life building his company, out of work. Each character comes to terms with the fact that they are not living in alignment with their true heartfelt desires and values. Edward winds up forming a partnership with the man he was about to put out of business, even though it will make him less money, and Vivian chooses to leave the profession.

In the end, Edward arrives at her apartment in a white limousine, and she calls down to him from her bedroom window. Like Rapunzel, Vivian is on the top floor apartment, and he climbs the ladder to get her. He even refers to her as "Princess Vivian."

"So what happened after he climbed up the tower and rescued her?" he asks.

"She rescued him right back," she replies.

These three films, *Mirror Mirror, Snow White and the Huntsman,* and *Pretty Woman* are modern versions of Snow White and Rapunzel. For this step, I thought I'd have a little fun with Cinderella. If you haven't already, download your Star Pack, where you'll find the short story, *Cinderella and the Ruby Slippers.* Go to www.STARinYourOwnLifeStory.com/StarPack. You'll also find trailers to all three movies, along with the final scene from *Pretty Woman.*

Character

For a truly effective screenplay, you must know your characters backward and forward. The moment you begin to imagine character relationships—how your character deals with his parents, his siblings, his coworkers, and all that—you start to explore the world of your story, and suddenly scenes begin to emerge.

As you research your character (context, culture, occupation), create details (attitudes, values, emotions), develop backstory (physiology, sociology, psychology), and establish personality and behavior, you start putting the character in different situations in your mind, and you begin to imagine him or her in the most mundane and most exciting moments of his life.

http://thescriptlab.com/screenwriting/character

Develop Your Character
Lead with Light

According to the psychologist Carl Jung, we share a collective unconscious. Unlike your personal unconscious, which contains the memories you accumulate during your lifetime, the collective unconscious is shared by all human beings and is inherited at birth. Contained in our collective unconscious are archetypes. If I were to describe someone as a princess, knight, vampire, prostitute, or victim, for example, you would receive a specific impression of their character. If you look back on the modern versions of Snow White, Rapunzel, and Cinderella, you can see all of those archetypes displayed in these stories.

In this step, *Develop Your Character, Lead with Light,* you'll be introduced to a variety of archetypes and their shadow and light aspects. One archetype in particular, the princess, will be reviewed in detail.

Caroline Myss, author of *Sacred Contracts* and creator of *Archetype Cards,* writes that we form an agreement before we are born to learn certain life lessons and meet particular people, and we bring into our personal psyche twelve archetypes. Each archetype has a light side and a shadow side, and our life lessons come from learning what our archetypes have to teach us about our own empowerment.

Our challenge is to overcome the shadow side of our archetypes and live in the light. If you look at movies that show a transformation of the main character, the protagonist will invariably follow this same pattern. In *Defending Your Life*, Daniel steps out of his shadow-victim to learn the lesson of that archetype; in other words, he takes center stage to become the inspiring hero of his life. In *Pretty Woman*, Vivian and

Edward step out of the shadow of the prostitute archetype by leaving professions that compromise their spirit. In the updated versions of *Snow White*, Snow White ditches the shadow aspects of the princess (passive, helpless) to become a warrior. Most movie characters transform by going from weak to strong, bad to good, unconscious to aware.

This step is about becoming more self-aware—more conscious of your own behavior as well as the impact other people's behaviors have on you. By becoming more aware of the archetypes that resonate strongly with you, you will be able to develop the kind of character who is able to take center stage and transform your life. You'll also begin to notice how the most difficult characters in your life hang out in the shadows of their archetypes. The more you notice it, the more accepting of them you'll become. That's not to say you'll like them, but that you'll spend less time trying to change them, and probably less time *with* them.

According to Myss, we have four primary survival archetypes: the victim, the prostitute, the saboteur, and the child. Our remaining eight are unique and play a stronger role than others, but every archetype can influence our thoughts, choices, and behavioral patterns. Archetypes contain lessons in personal growth. I've chosen the following additional archetypes for this step; the hero/heroine, vampire, knight, thief, queen, and warrior.

The Hero/Heroine

As the star in your own life story, you *are*, by default, the hero/heroine; however, you may be acting more like the victim. The hero/heroine makes a conscious choice to conquer fear, overcome obstacles, transform their life, and therefore, achieve their dreams. They choose to become more conscious and spiritually aware, and in doing so, become an inspiration to those around them. Notice how, in the modern versions of the fairy tales, instead of being passive victims, Snow White, Vivian, and Cinderella become the true heroines of their stories.

"Above all, be the heroine of your life, not the victim."

—Nora Ephron

Someone living on the shadow side of this archetype disempowers others in order to get what they want, like the person who steps on other people on their way to the top, or the boss who takes credit for other people's work. They may appear heroic, having solved the problem or come up with a great idea, but they've completely disempowered their staff in the process. Giving credit to their team member would empower that person and make them look good for their excellent management skills, but they have yet to learn this lesson. Think of Katherine Parker in the movie *Working Girl*. She steals Tess Parker's idea and tries to present it as her own, even going so far as to fire Tess to cover up her secret. This, of course, backfires in the end, when Tess gets promoted and Katherine gets the boot. In *Swimming with Sharks*, Buddy Ackerman does the same to his assistant, Gus, with disastrous consequences. They steal from others to appear heroic. In the fairy tales, it's the wicked queen and stepmother who live on the shadow side of this archetype. It doesn't get any more disempowering than stealing someone's heart (or future).

The Victim

The victim encourages you to stand up and take charge of your life, no matter how difficult it may be to overcome a personal challenge. Following the steps in this book is a declaration to the universe that you are learning from this archetype. To live on the shadow side of your victim archetype is to wallow in self-pity, live in the past, and refuse to move forward. I'm sure you know people like this. If you find yourself blaming other people, such as your antagonist, for your problems, there's a good chance you are being a victim. You can't get through this experience of life without being betrayed, brokenhearted, disappointed, or knocked down in some way. The question is, are you going to sit there, or are you going to get back up?

In the classic fairy tales, the princesses appear heroic in the end because they win the prince, but they never leave their victim stance. As helpless damsels, they wait to be rescued. That's why I love the updated versions of the fairy tales. The princesses literally move out of the shadow side of the victim (stuck in a castle, waiting to be rescued) and into the light.

The Prostitute

The word prostitute automatically conjures up images of a person who trades sex for money. But the archetype of the prostitute extends beyond just sex. The light side of this archetype alerts you to when you are giving your power away in order to survive. If you are living in the shadow of this archetype, you make material objects and physical security more important than your own personal empowerment. As you saw from *Pretty Woman*, Edward may not be an actual prostitute, but he's still playing out the shadow aspects of this archetype.

A woman who stays in a relationship that erodes her self-esteem because it meets her material and security needs is another example. Just because she's in a committed relationship, it doesn't mean she isn't living out the shadow prostitute.

Carmella Soprano from the HBO series, *The Sopranos* is a perfect example of the married prostitute. Even though she knows that her husband, Tony, is a gangster and adulterer—and it is clear that she chooses to turn a blind eye to the fact that her husband is much worse than a thief (i.e., he's a murderer and a psychopath)—she stays because she loves her fancy house and homemaker lifestyle. Her friend, a priest, also plays a part in keeping her stuck, since her Catholic faith treats divorce as the greatest sin of all. At one point, we think there's hope for her when she finally has enough and kicks Tony out of the house. She begins to step out of the shadow to create a life of her own. Carmella becomes liberated from the chains of her religious training and even has a brief romance with a schoolteacher. Unfortunately, she finds that being middle-aged, with no dependable income from Tony and no established career of her own, leaves her with bleak prospects for the future. She's the shadow damsel and he the shadow knight. She regresses into the shadow prostitute by choosing to stay in the marriage, even acknowledging and accepting Tony's philandering. She decides that staying is her best option, and because it's now a conscious choice, her emotional outlook is more positive. She's reached a level of acceptance.

I'm just glad it wasn't me.

You may have stayed in a job that made you miserable because of a paycheck; or you may have done things in your professional life that weren't in line with your values. When this happened, you may have tried to drown out your inner wisdom, which urged you to move on.

You can still be empowered in this archetype if you are staying in a bad job or relationship for security reasons, if breaking up or quitting now would be more harmful to your children than staying. However, it isn't a free pass to stay in a bad situation in perpetuity. It's a signal that you can't ignore what's going on. You need to take steps to change the situation. Get training, go back to school, or go to counseling. To be living on the light side is to acknowledge the reality of the situation. You can't just sit and wait for it to get worse; you can't allow your health to erode; and you can't fantasize that it will get better or that someone or something will swoop in on a white horse and rescue you. Put together your resume. Start networking and actively look for something else. Find things outside of work that bring you joy so that work (or the relationship) is no longer your life's central focus.

To live on the shadow side of this archetype is to make a conscious choice to stay in a bad situation, be a victim, and hand your ruby slippers over to the wicked witch. It is to admit that you'd rather never reach the Emerald City than have to walk the long, yellow brick road.

To live on the light side is to take the first step.

The Saboteur

In the fourth step, *Listen to Your Director, Lead with Courage*, we will examine the saboteur archetype in more detail. The saboteur alerts you to times when self-doubt or low self-esteem have the potential to block your ability to move forward in your life—issues of the third chakra. You literally sabotage yourself by listening to the voice of your inner film critic.

Your inner director will also alert you to when you are about to sabotage someone else. By becoming more aware of your inner director, you can overcome the shadow side of this archetype.

The Child

The child archetype can take on many aspects. Myss breaks down the child archetype into the following descriptions: divine, eternal, nature, orphan, and wounded.

Think of someone you know who is young in mind, body, and spirit, regardless of their age. They are displaying light traits of the eternal child. Now think of Peter Pan. Talk about playful! But you probably wouldn't want to marry him, because he refuses to grow up and be responsible.

Someone who lives on the light side of their wounded child archetype may help abused or neglected children. They've found a way to forgive their past and extend their support to others. Someone who lives on the shadow side may blame childhood wounds for their poor relationships as adults.

Dorothy is an example of the orphan child, as are the princesses Cinderella, Sleeping Beauty, Snow White, and Rapunzel. People who have the orphan child archetype may have lost their parents at a young age, but it could also apply to anyone who feels like they don't belong to their family of origin, as though they were placed there by mistake. On the light side, the orphan child develops independence at an early age. On the shadow side, it manifests itself as an inability to mature and a need to find a new family to feel at home with.

The Vampire

Metaphorically, the vampire is a character who romantically seduces someone and then feeds off them on a psychic level. In stories like *Dracula* and *Interview with a Vampire*, these characters need to drain the life out of others in order to exist.

In *Dracula*, it takes three bites before Dracula's victim becomes the undead—destined to walk the earth in search of blood (symbolic of the need to drain other people of their light in order to fill one's own dark void). His victim has several chances to see that she is in danger of losing herself in the relationship (in this case, literally dying), destined to a life of darkness if she doesn't pull herself away. She moves past the point of "seeing the light." (It's much like the modern-day victim of domestic violence. The battered woman can't leave because her survival has become dependent on him, not just physically, but emotionally, i.e., "I love him!") She ignored the blood-red flags. Of course, the allure is the initial passion and longing. Someone with a vampire-like energy about them is extremely focused in his attention and desire for one person. The drama of feeling needed by someone has an appeal, at least at first. What begins as the ultimate emotional affair turns physical, then lethal.

The purpose of the vampire archetype is to alert you to when someone or something is draining your life force. It shows you when you may be losing yourself and even risking your life—not necessarily in terms of living versus dying, but in terms of the life you've created or want to build. Recognize this archetype in others, but also in yourself. Be aware of when you are draining someone else's energy or taking advantage of them.

I once had to let go of a coaching client because she was an energy vampire. Where most of my clients loved to do most of the talking, I had to drag everything out of her. Yet, she she'd show up at the same time each week. I finally couldn't take it anymore. She was a nice person, but after every one of our meetings, I felt like I needed a blood transfusion.

The *Twilight* series highlights both the light and shadow aspects of the vampire. Although they claim vampires have no souls, Edward and the Cullen clan have made a conscious decision not to indulge the shadow aspects of their character by hunting animals instead of humans. The craving for human blood is still there, but they prove themselves capable of controlling it. They acknowledge the shadow aspects of their character, but choose to live in the light.

Bella, the heroine, is completely taken in by Edward. True to vampire form, she is the only one he wants. She chooses to give up her own mortality to be with him. She's his willing victim. Given that she's chosen to literally give up her life to be with Edward, she's also engaging in self-sabotage. She's got aspects of the orphan child, where you never get the sense that she feels like she belongs to her own family. She even refers to her father not as Dad but as Charlie, and she is all too eager to become part of the Cullen clan. There are also aspects of the nature child in Bella.

Girls look at Edward and Bella's love as their romantic ideal. And to have a Jacob there as a backup plan—an amazingly hot guy who adores you no matter how many times you reject him, well, who could ask for more? You've got one who can transform into a werewolf. He'll keep you from freezing to death by sleeping beside you in a tent in the middle of winter. You've got another who may be cold to the touch because he's technically dead, but he'll protect you and make passionate, break-the-bed love to you. Plus, he has no problem with you staying friends with another man who's in love with you too. It doesn't matter that you have strong feelings for him, because you love him more. Forget that Edward is a bit of a stalker.

My boys call *Twilight* a girl's movie. I can't tell you how often I hear people classify themselves or their significant others as being either an Edward or a Jacob. *Twilight* has definitely made an imprint on the way thousands of people view relationships, as if they weren't hard enough already.

The Queen from Snow White and the Huntsman is very much the vampire. She sucks the youth and beauty from her victims and tries to take Snow White's life. Watch the movie trailer in your Star Pack and you'll see what I mean. She also plays the femme fatale – the seductress who lures the king into marrying her and then kills him. Interesting that Kristen Stewart, who plays Bella in Twilight, was cast as Snow White in this movie.

The Knight

Ah, the knight. He's the one we dream of. He's the one coming to rescue us from all sorts of things—our single status, bad childhood, poverty, the need to work, the need to develop our character, or our plight in general. These are our own issues, however. A person displaying positive traits of the knight is romantic, chivalrous, and willing to go to great lengths to protect another's honor. These are wonderful qualities. Women who aren't in need of rescuing still desire an honorable, chivalrous man. Jacob and Edward from *Twilight* could be viewed as knights.

The shadow knight, however, is neither honorable nor chivalrous. He may present himself in a way that implies he's "saving" when in reality he's controlling. Similar to the abuser whose shadow vampire-like personality drains his victim of her life force, a shadow knight will keep his damsel weak and needy. He may highlight her imperfections and cause her to question her intelligence by making mountains out of molehills. An overdone steak becomes evidence of her poor cooking skills. The fact that you're female automatically makes you unable to make decisions of your own. He always knows what's best for you. He'll even find evidence to prove his case—ancient texts, for example. Any attempt made by his damsel to grow up and become more self-reliant is a threat to his ego.

The Thief

This one is pretty self-explanatory. A thief steals. In her shadow, the thief takes what isn't hers, just because she can. Rich investors taking over companies only to deplete them of their resources, regardless of the fact that they're already millionaires many times over, are thieves from an archetypal perspective—as depicted in Edward's character in *Pretty Woman*. The Katherine Parker and Buddy Ackerman characters are thieves. Gas companies that jack up prices during a crisis, people who overprice their services, and credit card companies that tack on 29% interest rates are all examples of stealing. Just because they can or because it's legal doesn't make it any less of an act of theft. Thieves steal other people's ideas, time, money, and affection. An adulterer, from an archetypal standpoint, is a thief.

It seems odd that vampires and thieves could possibly have a light side to them. The way I interpret the light side of the thief is the same way I see a vampire. It's an archetype that only becomes a behavior if we choose to let it. The urge to steal—whether it's another person's partner, idea, money, or time, is a sign that you need to have more faith in yourself and your ability to find your own mate, earn your own money, come up with your own ideas, and be patient. As Myss describes it in her Archetype Card, the light side "sheds light on the potential wealth within you that can never be stolen."

The Queen

The shadow side of the queen archetype is depicted in both the modern and classic versions of the fairy tales. She's seen as a lonely character who intimidates and controls to get what she wants, whether it's a literal queen, as is the case in Snow White, or a queen figure, like Cinderella's wicked stepmother. The queen is always depicted as a dark and evil force in these stories—a woman consumed by jealousy and rage, who will do whatever it takes to destroy anyone who gets in her way. The queen archetype represents female power and authority, whether it's in the home or at the office. A character who displays the lighter aspects of the queen archetype can be seen in the *Shrek* movies. I love a scene from *Shrek the Third* where the princesses are trapped in the castle. The queen literally "uses her head" to free the princesses from the castle prison. She's a benevolent leader who empowers and uplifts the women coming up behind her. Here's that scene:

Shrek the Third

```
Int. Castle
Princess Fiona and her mother, the Queen,
are trapped in a room with Cinderella, Snow
White, and a narcoleptic Sleeping Beauty.
They have been kidnapped by the narcis-
sistic Prince Charming and his scheming
mother, a fairy determined to find Charming
his princess. Rapunzel sold out along the
way and went with Charming.
Sleeping Beauty and Cinderella are
lounging.
Fiona and her mother are pacing, trying to
think of a way to escape.

                    FIONA
        We've got to find a way out now!

                 SNOW WHITE
        Ladies, assume your positions!
        Sleeping Beauty and Cinderella
        stand up. Sleeping Beauty bows her
        head and nods off again. Snow White
             and Cinderella do nothing.
```

```
                    FIONA
            What are you doing?

                SLEEPING BEAUTY
            Waiting to be rescued!

                    FIONA

                 (dismayed)
    It's time to take matters in our own hands!

                  SNOW WHITE
               We're just four...

Close on: The Queen

                  SNOW WHITE
    ...three hot princesses, two circus freaks,
        a pregnant ogre, and an old lady.

                    QUEEN
         Hmm. Old lady, coming through.

The queen turns to face the brick wall,
walks toward it, and knocks it down with
her head.
```

The Warrior

The fierce protector, the warrior is willing to go to battle for a cause, to protect family or way of life. Fighting for someone's rights is the mission of the warrior. A warrior is loyal and invincible. If you could imagine a storybook knight in shining armor, you may envision a handsome man sitting upon a white horse and extending his hand to "mi'lady." Edward from *Pretty Woman* is the knight, showing up in his white limousine to rescue Vivian. In contrast, the warrior may be a bit rougher around the edges and less concerned with impressing the "fairest in the land" or rescuing a damsel in distress. While the traditional image of the warrior is male, women have always been warriors as well. We will do anything to protect our children. We will speak up for women's rights and out against domestic violence. The Snow White characters in *Mirror Mirror* and *Snow White and the Huntsman* are warriors.

Erin Brockovich became the warrior in the movie of her life where she helped to win the largest settlement in US history on behalf of the people of Hinkley, California. Arguably one of the most inspiring films, and the one which earned Julia Roberts an academy award, *Erin Brockovich* is a wonderful example of what it means to step out of the shadow princess and victim archetypes to become a star—an inspiring leading lady, fierce protector, warrior, and queen.

The shadow warrior "distorts or abandons ethical principles and decency in the name of victory at any cost. What can be a virtue— heroic indifference to risk and pain—becomes contemptible when the indifference is directed not at oneself but at others" (http://www.myss. com/library/contracts/three_archs.asp).

The Princess

The traditional fairy tales *Rapunzel, Sleeping Beauty, Cinderella,* and *Snow White* manifest the princess archetype. Each story depicts a young woman stuck in her circumstances, dreaming of the day when her prince will come and save her. For too many of us, the princess archetype has had a big influence on the way we view work and love.

Each princess displays both the light and shadow aspects of this archetype. Think of the traits of the classic princesses. They are attractive, sweet, playful, happy, positive, hopeful, faithful, and kind. But they are also passive, repressed (they never get angry), and easily pushed around; they engage in wishful thinking, wait to be rescued, and lack assertiveness. On top of that, they hide their true feelings, which is represented in the metaphor of their living situations. Rapunzel is trapped in a castle; Sleeping Beauty is in the witness protection program, hiding in a cabin in the woods under a false identity (and then in a coma, in which she feels nothing). Cinderella is held hostage in an abusive home. And Snow White is forced into hiding with the seven dwarves (and then she, too, falls in a coma).

The message of the stories is that a happy life can be found through rescue by and marriage to Prince Charming, and in order to snag the prince, one must embody both these positive and negative traits. However, in reality, if you hide your true feelings, don't speak up, allow yourself to be pushed around, and conceal your true identity, it can have a disastrous effect on your ability to choose an appropriate mate, be in a healthy relationship, and live a meaningful life. It can also hold you back from achieving what you want in your professional life. If you live with the belief that a prince is out there, waiting to rescue you from your need to earn a living, then you may not put your best foot forward in your career.

Common to all of these stories is the fact that none of the girls has to do any inner work to escape their plight. There is no transformation of character. None of the girls ever has to stand up to injustice—just wait to be saved by a prince. If there's any transformation at all, it's entirely external, and done by someone else. In Cinderella's case, she is literally transformed before our eyes by her fairy godmother. She turns her tattered dress into a ball gown and her flats into glass slippers. In other words, a makeover was all she needed. It is through magic that the princesses find a resolution to their conflict. The answers are found outside themselves.

The answer to life's problems lies in their youth, beauty, and passivity. The men are their saviors, and evil, older women, their oppressors. There are no dark male characters in any of these stories.

The classic princess tales are appealing because they feed our wish to have things come to us through an outside source. But what if the prince never came? What if he turned out to be a nightmare? On what planet would someone grow up with such abuse and not suffer damage to her self-esteem? Who in her right mind would marry someone after a single dance? Wouldn't we be offended if a man could only identify us by our shoe size? The allure of these fairy tales is in the idea that you can get to your happy ending without doing any work, other than housework, gym workouts, and visits to the cosmetics counter. There's an ideal man out there who's not only completely smitten with us, but who is so desirable we will find passion in nothing else.

In *Inside Story, the Power of the Transformational Arc*, Dara Marks describes how having a character swoop in to save the day renders any effort done by the protagonist meaningless. This is classically referred to as a *deus ex machina* (the god from the machine), which means that the solution to the conflict comes from some unexpected outside source. The term comes from Greek tragedies, where a crane was used to lower actors playing gods onto the stage. The writer of *Pretty Woman* avoided a deus ex machina intervention—even though Edward "rescues" her in the end—because prior to his arrival, she'd chosen to rescue herself by making the decision to quit prostitution. The boy-meets-girl,-boy-loses-girl,-boy-gets-girl-in-the-end story is still intact without rendering Vivian's growth meaningless. That's why I love the modern fairy tales—they show an empowered female.

Although I will admit there are times I wish some guy would sweep me off my feet and make life easier…Okay, like all the time—I wish this all the time, I also know that I derive a lot of pleasure from *not* looking at men in this way. I think of it as preferring to wear the ruby slippers instead of a pair made of glass, as Cinderella does in my modern version. But I can still wear a pair of ruby slippers when he surprises me with a trip to a four-star, Mexican resort and a week of Edward-style passion. I've come across enough on-line dating profiles where men specifically write, "no princesses!" to understand that they don't want any of that nonsense either, but they still want to make a woman happy. I'm completely open to that.

Dorothy doesn't plunk herself down on the side of the yellow brick road and wait for her fairy godmother to appear and her prince to save her. She stays grounded in her personal power—her ruby slippers. She faces her fears, stands up to her antagonist, and walks the yellow brick road to find her own way home. She is the enlightened princess.

Are you living on the light or shadow side of the princess archetype? You may think you've moved on from this mindset because you have a career, and you're not waiting for a prince. But are you waiting to be rescued in other ways? For example, are you expecting others to promote you? Do you view your manager as someone who should speak for you? Do you look to your company to provide you with professional development opportunities? Are you waiting for the right politician to save the country, the economy, or other large-scale or even global situation, releasing you from having to do your part? Are you afraid of negotiating for better pay? Instead of accessing your courage, do you blame your boss or client when you don't get the compensation you feel you deserve?

> *"I always feel like there is some dude out there with money that I could fall back on if I needed to."*
>
> —*Kirstie Alley*

The Modern Princess's Transformation

ACT 2

Mind
Believes in herself

Heart
Loves herself

Courage
Stands up for herself

ACT 1

ACT 3

Challenge:
Imprisoned by evil
oppressor or circumstance

Resolution:
Takes the lead
Finds true love

Summary

In the movie of your life, you are the screenwriter. You have the ability to identify the archetypal patterns that have influenced your character the most so far, and work with her to transform her life and achieve her vision by embracing the light side of her archetypes. Which archetypes resonate most with you? In the upcoming steps you will continue to develop your character and help her figure out which archetypes hold her back, and which to embrace to help her get ahead.

If you find the study of archetypes as fascinating as I do, then be sure to join the *Star in Your Own Life Story* course. You'll have an opportunity to explore your archetypes in more detail. Visit www.STARinYourOwnLifeStory.com/course.

Notes

STEP THREE

Become a Producer

Lead with Sovereignty

Gone with the Wind

SCARLETT

I'm sorry Ashley, but have you forgotten what
it's like without money? I found out that
money's the most important thing in the world.
I don't intend ever to be without it again.
I'm going to make money and that's so the
Yankees can never take Tara away from me, and
I'm going to make it the only way I know how.

ASHLEY

But we're not the only Southerners
who've suffered, Scarlett. Look at all
of our friends. They're keeping their
honor and their kindness too.

SCARLETT

Yes, and they're starving. I have no use
for anyone who won't help themselves. Oh,
I know what they're saying about me, and
I don't care. I'm going to make friends
with the Yankee carpetbaggers, and I'm
going to beat them at their own game, and
you're going to beat them with me.

Gone with the Wind

Scarlett O'Hara (Vivien Leigh) is the oldest of three girls and enjoys the plantation life of the Old South, but her life of luxury, complete with slaves who work the cotton fields and who cater to her every whim as house servants at Tara, is about to end.

In the opening scene of this epic film, sixteen-year-old Scarlett is flirting with the Tarleton twins on her veranda. They're talking about a barbecue they'll be attending at the Wilkes's plantation, Twelve Oaks. Scarlett finds out that the man she has her heart set on marrying, Ashley Wilkes (Leslie Howard), is going to propose to his cousin, Melanie Hamilton (Olivia de Havilland). This sets up Scarlett's act 1 challenge and a theme throughout the film. Ashley becomes her obsession, her conquest. From then on, her primary focus and mission in life is to win his heart. Virtually all of her decisions are filtered through her infatuation with him.

Scarlett attends the party at Twelve Oaks, and sure enough, Ashley announces his engagement to Melanie. This is also where she meets Rhett Butler (Clark Gable) for the first time, a man who becomes Scarlett's antagonist, and later in the story, her leading man.

Rhett has a questionable reputation. He's a savvy businessman who adapts to the changing South with a primary allegiance to himself, not the Confederacy.

Rhett is immediately taken by Scarlett. Unlike the other girls, she is bold, brazen, and a shameless flirt. She understands the power she has over men, and she uses it to her advantage. When all the other girls are taking an afternoon nap, she sneaks downstairs to confront Ashley and declare her love for him. Ashley expresses his fondness for Scarlett, as he does throughout the film, but as an honorable man and a practical person, he knows that he and Scarlett would never be a good match. Ashley seems to be the only man unwilling to give Scarlett what she wants.

Rhett embarrasses Scarlett when he reveals his presence after her confession is over, Ashley has left the room, and she's smashed a piece of china against the wall. Throughout the movie, Rhett is the one person who calls Scarlett on her nonsense. He sees and appreciates her for who she really is. This unnerves Scarlett, yet intrigues her at the same time.

Scarlett overhears the other girls speaking poorly about her, but Melanie Hamilton, "Melly," the woman whom Ashley is going to marry, comes to her defense. Melanie likes Scarlett's spirit, and is consistent in her love for her throughout the story. Rejected by the women and by Ashley, but determined to make a life for herself in spite of all of them, Scarlett manipulates Melanie's brother, Charles, into proposing to her on the same day.

That very afternoon, the war starts, and the men rush to enlist in the Confederate army. Charles Hamilton dies of pneumonia in training camp. Scarlett's sorrow isn't over his death, but over having to wear black and feeling like her life is over at such a young age. Her mother sends her to Atlanta to stay with Melanie and her Aunt Pittypat.

Mammy, her maid since birth, is a constant support for Scarlett. She knows Scarlett's real motive is to be there when Ashley comes home on leave. The judgment is on her face, but she still stands by Scarlett's side.

At a benefit in Atlanta, Scarlett meets Rhett again. In a playful auction, Rhett offers one hundred and fifty dollars for a dance with Scarlett—a scandal, since she's in mourning. She's thrilled, and while they're dancing, he tells her, "With enough courage, you can do without a reputation." He tells her he looks forward to the day when she says she loves him. She says it will never happen as long as she lives.

He buys her a green hat, and although she's still technically in mourning, she wears it. In a memorable moment and classic movie line, Rhett pulls her close. Scarlett closes her eyes and bends her head back.

Rhett says, "No, I don't think I will kiss you, although you need kissing, badly. That's what's wrong with you. You should be kissed—often, and by someone who knows how."

Their relationship is the most interesting in the film, and over time it becomes clear that he is her perfect match. He sees it, and we see it, but Scarlett can't see it; Rhett says he is waiting for her to grow up and get Ashley out of her heart.

Ashley comes home on furlough and a brokenhearted Scarlett must witness his devotion to Melanie. As he's leaving, he asks Scarlett to look after Melly because, as he puts it, she is frail and gentle. She agrees, to please him, and then she throws herself at him. He kisses her but then pulls away. She tells him she loves him and confesses to marrying Charles only to upset him. Throughout the story, Ashley leaves the impression that he is with Melanie for practical and honorable reasons and never sets a clear boundary for Scarlett, which leaves her hoping that she somehow still has a chance with him.

Melanie and Scarlett nurse the wounded Confederate soldiers. Belle Watling, a prostitute, offers to make a donation (the money is tied in a handkerchief with Rhett Butler's initials on it) to the hospital. Melanie treats her with respect, but Scarlett treats her with disdain.

On the day the Union Army is flooding into Atlanta, Melly goes into labor, but no doctors are available—they are tending the wounded. Prissy, their maid, finally confesses that she "don't know nothin' 'bout birthin' babies," so Scarlett takes charge and delivers the baby. She summons Rhett Butler to rescue them from the inferno of Atlanta, but he stops short of Tara. He knows Scarlett can make it the rest of the way. It's one of the things I like about him. Rhett likes a strong woman. When she objects to his leaving and tries to make him feel ashamed for abandoning a "helpless woman," he laughs, "You, helpless? Heaven help the Yankees if they capture *you*."

He climbs down and then asks her to kiss him goodbye. She resists, so he grabs her around the waist, pulls her toward him, and declares his love for her. "Because we're alike—bad lots, both of us. We're selfish and shrewd, but able to look things in the eyes and call them by their right names."

Scarlett slaps him for kissing her against her wishes. You can't help but love the grin on Rhett's face as she acts offended, but man that had to hurt. She keeps rejecting him, and he's, well...he's Clark Gable for crying out loud! Wake up and smell the coffee, Scarlett! I mean, seriously—Ashley? *Ashley*? Oh my God, what I wouldn't do...

But Scarlett won't allow herself to love Rhett Butler. She continues to hold out for the unavailable, Southern gentleman, Ashley Wilkes.

Rhett hands her a gun for protection, then walks off to join the retreating Confederate army.

They reach Twelve Oaks first and find it destroyed, but ever pragmatic, she tells Prissy to tie a stray cow to the back of the wagon. At Tara, she discovers that the Yankees have stolen everything. Her mother died the night before, and her father, stunned by the loss of his beloved wife, has succumbed to dementia.

At the end of Part One, Scarlett makes her way in the dark to the ravaged garden. She plucks a single carrot left in the ground and collapses from hunger and exhaustion, but she doesn't stay down for long. Scarlett pulls herself together and stands up, fist in the air, and declares, "As God as my witness, they're not going to lick me. I'm going to live through this, and when it's all over, I'll never be hungry again—No, nor any of my folk. If I have to lie, cheat, or kill, as God as my witness, I'll never be hungry again." (You can view the scene in your Star Pack.)

This is a turning point for Scarlett and marks the time when she truly steps into her role as a grown woman. They are penniless and hungry. Scarlett and her two sisters sow and pick their own cotton, and Scarlett is hardheaded and determined to bring her family through the war. When a Yankee deserter enters her home, she kills him with the gun Rhett gave her. Up to this point, she sees Melanie as the person who stands in the way of her having Ashley, but she gains respect for her when she appears, still weak from childbirth, at the top of the stairs dragging a sword. The two women take the man's money and Scarlett buries his body out back. She acknowledges the fact that she's committed murder but says, "I won't think about that now. I'll think about that tomorrow." That is Scarlett's mantra. It's her way of avoiding painful truths and forging ahead.

The war ends and Melanie and Scarlett look forward to Ashley's return. But Scarlett's first reaction is, as ever, a practical one: "We'll plant more cotton. Cotton ought to go sky high next year," she says.

Scarlett is becoming a real producer—taking the reins of her own life and sovereignty over her family's affairs. Gone with the wind are the days when Scarlett would just assume money would be there for her. She has stepped into her role as the leading lady, not just a belle of the ball.

When she finds out that the carpetbaggers have raised the taxes on Tara, she goes to see Ashley.

Ashley calls himself a coward. Life has become too real for him. He says that he finds himself in a world that's worse than death—a world in which there's no place for him. "What do you think becomes of people when their civilization breaks down? Those who have brains and courage come through all right. Those that haven't are winnowed out."

He acknowledges Scarlett's fearlessness. When she begs him to tell her he loves her, he tells her he loves her courage and her stubbornness, but he isn't going to forget the best wife a man could ever have. He reminds her that there is something she loves better than him: Tara.

Scarlett decides that Rhett may be her best bet for getting the money she needs. She sashays into the Yankee jail wearing a green velvet dress, putting on airs, and flirting with Rhett, but her rough hands reveal the truth of her desperate situation. Rhett rejects her for lying to him.

As she is on her way out, Belle Watling walks in.

Scarlett discovers that her sister Suellen's beau, Frank Kennedy, is running a successful shop in Atlanta and has a "sideline" lumber business. Scarlett sees the potential in the lumber yard and seizes the opportunity almost immediately. She lies to him and says that Suellen plans to marry another man. Before you know it, Scarlett is Frank Kennedy's wife, and she's writing a check for three hundred dollars to the tax collector.

Scarlett has just become the sacred prostitute. She's sold herself into marriage in order to save her home. Belle Watling is Scarlett's antithesis. She is honest in her prostitution, but Scarlett's willingness to marry for money is just prostitution in a more socially acceptable form.

Scarlett married first for revenge and now for money. Naturally, Suellen is beside herself, and Ashley is humiliated. Scarlett manipulates him into staying to help run the lumber business, even getting the naïve Melanie to back her up because of everything Scarlett's done for them. Ashley is a beaten man, a metaphor for the South.

Scarlett proves to be a better businesswoman than any man, including her husband. She is the scandal of Atlanta for running a business. She collects on his customer's outstanding debts and hires convicts at the lumber mill. Ashley objects to using convicts, but she responds with the lines that opened this chapter. She hasn't forgotten what it's like without money, doesn't care what people think, and intends to beat the Yankees at their own game.

Really what she is doing is learning how the game is played, and instead of fighting it, she's playing it and playing it well.

The women about town are also appalled that she drives her own buggy and that she's doing business with the very people who destroyed the south, but she doesn't care. Scarlett is adapting to the new South, and seizing every opportunity she can to ensure her family's welfare.

You go, girl.

Of course, when Rhett Butler buys his way out of jail and bumps into her downtown, he's quick to call her on her propensity for marrying people she doesn't love, which she doesn't like one bit. She takes off in her buggy.

Rhett places his hat on his head and says with admiration, "What a woman!"

The Role of a Producer

"Hollywood's most successful type of movie producer realizes that raising money is essential to making movies. Though she uses her influence and connections to bolster her projects, she realizes that the most essential component of her career description is the ability to make financially sound decisions. When mounting a film project, any smart movie producer asks herself, 'Will this film be profitable?'"

http://www.sparknotes.com/lit/gonewith/themes.html

Become a Producer
Lead with Sovereignty

C ouples fight about money. People marry for money. They stay in bad relationships for money and trade sex for money (both in and out of relationships). They base their decisions about whether or not to do something they enjoy not just on what it costs, but on whether or not it will result in financial gain. In *Gone with the Wind*, Scarlett O'Hara certainly based many of her decisions on money and security, as well as her infatuation with Ashley Wilkes. Her survival instincts were strong when she let her rational self make the decisions; when she listened only to her heart, she screwed up every time.

In this chapter, you are going to see how money, sex, and creativity are interconnected, so that you can become more conscious of how you may have allowed your thoughts and beliefs in this area to hold you back, and how you can use this powerful energetic connection to move you forward.

Money in and of itself is neither good nor bad. It's simply a method of exchange. None of us can get along without it. Why don't we just admit it? Money is important. Most of us could use more of it. Not only do we need it to survive, but with extra money, we can travel, purchase luxuries, and enjoy some of the good things in life that actually *are* things. What's wrong with that?

I know people who live close to the poverty line and pride themselves on needing as little as possible to survive. They view life's luxuries as wasteful and think they are better than those who, in their minds, waste money on unnecessary things. Instead of experiencing life as abundant, they have a consciousness of poverty and lack—a there-is-only-so-much-to-go-around mentality.

I also have friends who drive BMWs, live in gorgeous homes, and travel on a regular basis. They're always looking for ways to maximize their income so that they can live a more lavish lifestyle and have more to give. They had a greater vision for their lives and understood early on the difference between getting a job and establishing a career or business. They value their time and talents and expect others to do so as well. They are generous. They have an abundance mentality.

And then there are those of us who are somewhere in between.

As I write this, we've been listening for years to messages that tell us how bad the economy is. What's the economy if not money? And what's money if not power? And who is in charge of the economy, anyway? We may not feel as though we have an impact on the national or global economy, although we certainly play a part. We do have control over our own economy, the economy of our individual and family finances.

In home economics class, I often thought the purpose of it was to learn how to bake pinwheel cookies and sew buttons on a shirt. That took care of the home part, but we were given nothing to satisfy the economics part. I don't remember learning much of anything about income versus expenses, debits versus credits, jobs versus careers, checking versus savings accounts, business ownership versus employment, and investments versus liabilities. We may have Suze Orman and Robert Kiyosaki talking openly about money now, but somewhere along the way, talking about money was deemed unseemly. Taboo. Like politics and religion, you're not supposed to discuss it, especially the joy of it. It's not taught in schools, and yet it's an important life skill—how to make it, keep it, invest it, donate it, and have a little fun with it, too. People avoid their money until it becomes a huge problem.

How much you make, whether or not you make as much as someone else doing the same thing, how much you're taxed, who benefits from those taxes, the price of gas, who gets what—money, money, money. If it weren't important, we wouldn't be concerned with any of these things.

Money matters.

This isn't about greed, but about enjoying everything life has to offer. Having disposable income gives you a sense of security. If you don't think money is important, just ask someone who doesn't have enough or who's in debt up to their eyeballs. I guarantee you it's what they focus on the most, far more than someone with an abundance of it. A person with disposable income doesn't have to make it their primary focus, at least not in the sense that they have to worry about paying the bills, but the poor person certainly does.

As Robert Kiyosaki, author of the *Rich Dad, Poor Dad* books, once said, there are two kinds of money problems—too much and too little. I know which problem I'd like to have. Like Scarlett O'Hara, who decided she was going to beat the carpetbaggers at their own game, Kiyosaki advocates for learning the way money works and adapting to the reality of money.

This chapter isn't just about money, but money plays a huge role in our lives when it comes to our relationships, our careers, and even our creative pursuits. Think about your attitude toward money. Did you grow up with parents who told you rich people were selfish? It's pretty hard to build wealth with that belief stuck in your head, because to attract wealth means being a bad person. Did they look down on people who weren't as well-off as they were? Then your belief may be that you have to marry a rich person, lest you be looked down upon. We have books on how to live frugally and books on how to make millions. It seems money isn't the problem. It's our attitude towards it. As I once told my brother, who referred to someone as a "rich asshole", there are rich jerks and poor jerks. The money is irrelevant. No wonder we struggle.

I believe the more rights women have, and the more they exercise those rights, the more freedom everyone experiences. Relationships become more about love and compatibility than survival; careers are not only ways to earn an income, but a way to express our talents; creativity is an expression of the human spirit with value in and of itself, rather than something that is tossed aside as unimportant simply because it may not result in monetary gain—at least directly. I happen to believe that creativity for creativity's sake creates success in other areas. I know that all of the promotions I received at work came on the heels of a writing project.

If money is the root of all evil, then it's because it's made the primary reason to marry someone, take a job, start a war, sue somebody, or even decide whether or not you'll go on a weekend retreat or take an art class, regardless of whether or not you can paint like Van Gogh. I believe that to marry someone thinking money is unimportant is as much a mistake as it is to marry someone thinking it's the only thing that matters. Much better to partner up with a person who is a grown-up about it, knows how to talk about it, and who shares your same goals, drive, and attitudes about financial management. But first, you need to get your own house in order, regardless of your relationship goals.

The following stories share some commonalities regarding finances—from unrealistic expectations in relationships, dependency, entitlement, a failure to listen to intuition, and secrecy, to socially engrained, disempowering beliefs, denial, and guilt.

My Story

My ex-husband, Steve, was always smiling. That's how I think of him whenever I reminisce about the times when we first met. I worked at the Queen Executive Center, an office building where I held a part-time job as a receptionist on my summer break from college. He'd just gotten out of the Air Force and went to work with his father. I was only twenty years old, just a few months shy of my twenty-first birthday, and I still think of that time in my life as one of the happiest. Steve made me laugh. He was a hard worker, he was generous, he was fun, and it wasn't long before I fell in love.

We dated until I got out of college, and then I moved in with him. A few years later, we were married, and within four years, Jack and Christopher were born, making us a family of four. As most people do, we entered into marriage with faith that love would carry us through, but as many of us also learn over time, things happen, you grow apart, you learn things about yourself and the other person that you didn't know before, or didn't know were important, and we wound up divorced. I could fill a whole other book explaining why, but since this chapter is about becoming a producer, I'll focus on one of the things that contributed to the demise of our relationship: money.

Two weeks after we got home from our honeymoon, I received a phone call from a collection agency. It turned out Steve had a lot of credit card debt. We'd lived together for years but never talked about it. We maintained separate checking accounts, and I thought he paid his bills in full each month. When the family business struggled to stay afloat during the recession, he stopped taking home a paycheck and paid his bills with credit cards. I wasn't happy about it, but things happen, so I immediately offered to help him pay it off. He insisted he would take care of it himself.

When I found out he was often late paying the mortgage, I offered to take on the job of paying the household bills.

I thought we'd file a joint tax return now that we were married, but he told me that his accountant said it was better if we filed separately. Even though the tax specialist at H&R Block told me that "married filing separately" is the worst tax bracket to be in, he insisted she was wrong. Something in my gut told me that what he said wasn't right, but I believed him. When our relationship turned sour years later, I found out that he was behind on his taxes, and by the time we separated, he owed for about four years. He said he allowed it to get away from him, and he was too embarrassed to tell me. I was frustrated—because I could have had more money taken out of my paycheck each week to cover all of our taxes—but I loved him. I was confident we'd figure out a way to fix it. But it wasn't my problem to fix. It was his, and he didn't want me involved.

And such is the frustration of every married person alive— even though you're in a relationship with a person who is not you, according to the law, you are often held responsible for their actions. Or as the creditor who'd called me years earlier said, "When you married your husband, you married his debt."

Needless to say, we fought over money. If I brought up my concerns over his unpaid taxes, he'd call me a nag. I worried that the IRS would take our house away to settle his debt, but he seemed too overwhelmed to deal with it. If I mentioned my desire to move into a bigger house someday, he took it to mean I didn't appreciate how hard he worked or what we had. In a moment of frustration he said, "I have no desire to share my financial life with you."

Money was a sore subject in our house, because we didn't view it the same way. I just assumed we'd handle our finances together, but he wanted to keep that aspect of his life separate from mine. Because we were married, I knew what we did had an impact on us both, so my initial reaction was to always jump in and take over. In some ways it protected me, but in others, it probably didn't help our relationship. I could feel him growing resentful, and it had an impact on us in the bedroom, too. I believe we both did the best we could at the time. This is life. But looking back, what I loved about him—his fun-loving personality and carefree attitude—became a problem when the responsibilities of family life came into play.

Steve and I didn't do our homework before we married each other, and there were a lot of things I didn't know about him that came back to bite me later. After we separated, his father's new wife sued us. Steve and I had agreed I'd keep our house since it was our boys' home. She tried to take it to settle one of Steve's old debts. He'd purchased the house from her several years before we were married, and neither of them were up front about the money he still owed her or the true nature of their agreement. (I was kept in the dark about a lot of things, but you knew that already.)

The details of this story are too big to go into here, so let me put it this way. She thought that marrying my father-in-law was her ticket to a secure future. A man was her financial plan, but when she found out he wasn't as wealthy as she thought, she sued us—or me, really, since the house was technically mine.

I often felt guilty not helping my ex-husband, but this time, I wasn't going to do it. I refused. I'd come to realize I had been a codependent wife, and that needed to change. It was a real act of will to hold him accountable instead of jumping in to take over. My experience taught me a valuable lesson in believing in myself and my intuition. After years of trying to work with him, I finally decided to stand my ground and let him figure it out, or in this case, allow the court to do its job.

That experience reinforced something I'd learned early on, and that was the importance of ensuring I am always a good producer of my life. My parents were schoolteachers, and I was one of five children, so money was tight. "We can't afford it" was a common phrase in my house. As a result, I became incredibly resourceful. I started making my own money when I was ten. I babysat until I was old enough to get a job. I paid for most of my own clothes. I watched as my mother's friends got divorced and were forced to move back in with their parents; some remarried—again to men who weren't right for them—for financial security. They never went to college or had any real job training, so their earning power was limited. I also learned at a young age how much I hated jobs. I knew that part of living a happy life meant finding a career—work that had meaning and that would provide an outlet for my talents (at least most of the time) and allow me to grow and become better off financially over time, so I made sure I got an education. Having a skillset is absolutely essential. I'd probably be stuck in a bad marriage if I hadn't been able to earn a living.

Growing up in this environment was incredibly beneficial in that it taught me the importance of financial independence. My father is a wonderful man, and he was an excellent provider. We just weren't rich, so although my needs were met, I knew that if I was going to have some of the nonessential things I wanted, I'd have to work for them.

I don't equate a person's value with the size of their bank account. But I didn't realize until later in life that I carried around the belief that wanting a man who was financially secure, generous, responsible, and an equal partner would be asking too much. I still felt like I had to go it alone in order to survive, so I refused to acknowledge my intuition about whether or not a man would be a good match for me when it came to my goals outside of love and romance. I attracted a man who didn't want to share his financial life with me. Is it any surprise? My husband, my lover, my friend, and the man who would become the antagonist of my life story, was my greatest teacher. He taught me that my needs matter, and that it's okay to desire a relationship with a person who wants to connect with me on a deep level.

My next relationship got me closer to that goal, but I still hadn't dealt with the money piece.

I think back on that time and how absurd it was. I exchanged a spendthrift for a cheapskate. Either way, I was the one left with the tab, but it's what I attracted. By stepping into my role as leading lady, I had no choice but to stop being a doormat.

I maintain personal sovereignty over my finances and always will, not just in having a career, but in keeping an eye out for when others are trying to take advantage of me or I'm not valuing myself enough. It's a lesson I've had to relearn as a business owner. Like everyone, I am a work in progress.

By the time my husband and I divorced, the lawsuit was over, and I ended the relationship with Joe, it had been ten years of strife. When the boys and I moved into our new home in 2004, I slept on the couch for two weeks before my new bed arrived. In spite of the fact that my back hurt, I crossed my hands in back of my head and slept more soundly than I had in a decade. From that moment on, I vowed that my home would be a peaceful, happy, secure, and creative place for my boys to grow up in. If I ever marry again, I will insist on full disclosure of all financially-related information beforehand, have a conversation with him about our beliefs and our goals regarding career and money, and make sure we are on the same page. He will be financially responsible but generous at the same time.

There's nothing you can do if someone lies to you, but when something feels off, you can heed your intuition and do the best you can. I understand the importance of maintaining sovereignty over my career and finances, and I hope the stories in this chapter help you to see the importance as well. Listen to your instincts. They are always accurate. And don't settle for anything less than what you truly desire in work or in love, because marriage is a contract, careers take years to build, and even if they fail to last a lifetime, they can have lifelong impacts.

As I write this, it's hard to believe that Steve and I have been divorced for close to thirteen years. He's now got a thriving business, and our boys are in high school. We learn from everyone we come in contact with in life, but the hardest lessons come from our soul mates. I thank God for my relationship with Steve, even though there were some painful moments. He's the father of my children, and as a result of knowing him, I learned to trust my intuition and discovered my love for writing. And not only that, but as a gift, he contributed to the production of this book.

When you read about the second chakra, you'll be able to reflect on these stories to see how money, sex, and creativity/work are intimately connected. For now, here are a few more case studies.

Melissa's Story

Melissa almost didn't want to tell me her story because of the shame she felt. Throughout her twenty-year marriage, she had a higher income than her husband. As a successful investment banker, she brought in over three hundred thousand dollars a year. Her husband convinced her to put all of their assets in his name. He also convinced her it would be smart to keep all the liabilities in hers. Like many of us, she believed in her marriage and tried to overlook the way he treated her, until she found out he was on Match.com. When they divorced, she was completely wiped out and he got everything, including their friends, because he managed to convince them he was the one who'd been mistreated. She's angry, but she's reinventing her life. I have no doubt she will, given her track record for earning. Even highly educated, intelligent women fall into this trap.

Alison

Alison seemed to have the ideal relationship, complete with the cute nicknames. After their children were born, she found out her "Snookums" had been seeing a woman at work. For years, she sat back and watched him purchase every as-seen-on-TV gadget until their credit card debt totaled over one hundred thousand dollars. He had a good job, but she made close to double his pay. Still, losing his income and having to take on half their debt with two babies in daycare was no easy task.

Amanda's Story

I knew my friend Amanda was in trouble when I asked her if she and her husband John had taken advantage of the low interest rates by refinancing their home. They'd bought their house on a variable interest rate, so it would have been a good move for them. Amanda's eyes glazed over at the mere mention of money and bills. She let her husband take care of those things.

Eight years later, it turns out that John's way of handling their finances was to make up for the loss in household income by paying bills on credit. He thought he'd catch up later, and he wanted to be the man and provider who spared his wife financial discomfort. He never refinanced their mortgage, and when the housing bubble burst, their interest rate went through the roof and made their monthly payment unaffordable. They lost all their equity (after twelve years) when they had to short-sell their home and were forced to move into a rental property. Their sex life is nearly nonexistent. She just doesn't feel like it. But Amanda knows she was just as much to blame for their situation.

Many of us start out wearing a pair of glass slippers. My hope is that you'll stand in your power and wear the ruby ones instead.

Through our thoughts, feelings, and beliefs—our energy and vibration—we attract all of this. We attract based on where we are and what we know, feel, and believe. This isn't a bad thing. It's life. Until we are clear about what we truly want, we feel it, and we believe it's possible, we will continue to attract these types of people and situations. And how we think, the choices we make, has an impact on our second chakra.

The Second Chakra: Sacral

The second chakra, or sacral chakra, is located in your abdominal area and corresponds to your lower back, hips, inner thighs, womb, genitals, the skin, and the senses (eyes, ears, nose, and mouth). Where the root chakra relates to your sense of survival in the world, your sacral chakra relates to your ability to enjoy the world through sensuality, sexuality, and creativity. Its element is water, and its color is orange. Money, sex, and creativity all relate to your second chakra. To have a balanced second chakra is to have balanced emotions and to be able to go with the flow. The demon of the second chakra is *guilt*.

Becoming a producer of your life story means maintaining personal sovereignty over your creative life, your career, and your finances. It's about living in the light side of your archetypes, such as the victim, the prostitute, and the princess. The princess archetype is especially powerful in the second chakra. Even those of us who grew up understanding the importance of having a career may still be wearing glass slippers when it comes to blindly trusting a partner, abdicating responsibility to them, or falling into the trap of a father/daughter dynamic instead of a partnership.

Many women who are out-earning their partners still think they need a man to survive. I'm not saying we don't need men or that we don't want them to be good providers. I love men and want men to act like men. What I'm saying is that we are fortunate to be living in a time when we don't need to consider our survival prospects when we decide whom to marry, yet so many people fail

> *"You have to learn the rules of the game. And then you have to play better than anyone else."*
>
> *—Albert Einstein*

to take care of themselves in this regard. Failure to build a career or have a skillset is dangerous. Even if you decide to stick with traditional gender roles in your relationship, you'd better make sure you and he agree that a) whatever income he brings in is considered yours as a couple and b) decisions are made together. I think there are enough examples out there of women who have completely abdicated responsibility for their financial lives with disastrous consequences. Same goes for men. In my book *Stuck with Mr. Wrong*, I tell Jim's story. He was very much the knight, but he allowed his chivalrous nature to go too far when he allowed his girlfriend to mooch off of him and spend his money to the point where he lost his house.

Money and creativity are like aphrodisiacs when they are flowing in a healthy way. People who are artistic and who enjoy abundance are highly attractive and sought-after mates. Even those who wouldn't normally get a second glance suddenly become attractive when they are on top of their game. On the other hand, a beautiful woman or handsome man can be a complete turnoff when they look to their mates to be their be-all, end-all, have no outside interests, or harm their partners financially.

Financial irresponsibility can be a real relationship killer, and it certainly can ruin a couple's sex life when debt becomes overwhelming. Sixty percent of all erectile dysfunction is psychological.

Someone with a healthy, balanced, second chakra is able to express themselves, enjoy their romantic and sexual life, and be creative—whether through work, hobbies, art, or another pursuit—and live within their means with full awareness of their financial status.

Second Chakra Messages

I'm sure you can already tell what physical symptoms indicate when someone may be living with imbalance in this area. Look for sexual problems—impotency or low drive, promiscuity, lack of passion in creative pursuits, creative stagnation, low back pain, and other physical problems in the areas listed in this section.

Your Old South

In many ways, Scarlett's love for Ashley in *Gone with the Wind*, her love for something that wasn't real, was her love for the old way of life—a ghost. It was an attachment to the Old South, before the Civil War. Ashley admitted to being unable to adapt to the new way of life. He loved Melly, a wonderful but physically weak woman who eventually dies as a result of a miscarriage. The Old South is dead and buried.

What is your "Old South"? If you look at these characters as metaphors for holding onto something disempowering, like a belief system or a thought process that no longer serves your life story—an old and dying way of life, can you see where you may be holding onto an ideal that isn't real? Does it require the hard work and effort of others—

whether it's through government support, a knight in shining armor, or a belief that someone else is supposed to provide for you (like a slave)? In what ways does this keep you weak? How is all of this holding you back from writing a better script for your life?

Your New South

Rhett Butler represents the new South, and a metaphor for the freedom and passion that came from freeing the slaves and forming a new economy. He adapts and changes and does what he pleases, something that Scarlett does as well, yet she fights her upbringing, the lure of the easy lifestyle, and the social customs she grew up with. That is her true conflict over loving Ashley and her attraction, yet resistance, to loving Rhett. When she finally lets Ashley go, it's like fully letting go of the Old South, her old beliefs, and her entitled lifestyle. Opening her heart to Rhett is an opening to the New South. Where Ashley was weak, Rhett was strong and a good match for Scarlett's strength. But Scarlett adapted first in her courage in the face of all she had to do, then in her mind around women's place in society and what she could do for her family by choosing not to care what other people thought and running a business and her life on her own terms. In many ways, her love for Ashley is what got her through the hardships of war and its aftermath. Even though it was a childish infatuation, by her own admission it was what she lived for. It saw her through. The tragedy was that she was too late in realizing her true love for Rhett. She became so determined never to be poor, that she became imbalanced in her pursuit of money, although her optimism leaves you hoping that if there was a sequel, she would have found a way to get him back. In fact there was, and she did.

At the end of part one, she even reaches into the earth to pluck the last carrot from the garden and declares to God she'll never go hungry again.

Scarlett continually connects with the earth. She grounds herself in the face of fear of what's to come of her by remembering Tara. The first chakra is your center of survival, and its demon is fear. Throughout the film, Scarlett continually finds her courage and strength by grounding herself in reality and doing what needs to be done. She stays tight inside her ruby slippers and refuses to relinquish them to any antagonistic force that tries to stand in her way—whether it's a man, the war, the Yankee carpetbaggers, poverty, or social convention. It's what she does right up to the very end. Interesting that in the end, it is land that comforts her. But it's her relationship to money and men that provide the greatest conflicts throughout the story.

One of the most inspiring and memorable characters ever portrayed in film, Scarlett defied convention as an independent mind when women's choices were limited. She did what she had to do in order to survive and protect her land and the people in her care in the war-torn South, in spite of anyone else's opinions. She was flawed, she was beautiful, and she was ruthless, but she was a fighter and a survivor. For those of you who have ever had bag-lady fears, felt guilty about wanting more financial security (or had trouble visualizing it), think it's selfish to desire a mate who is a good earner, or conversely, believe a man is a good financial plan; or if you're afraid to negotiate better pay, fail to charge enough for your services, or think that living on the edge of survival is somehow divinely written into your life script, I encourage you to read or watch *Gone with the Wind*. Scarlett O'Hara may have been an imperfect character, but it's her imperfections that make her all the more inspiring, because we are all flawed. Her courage, tenacity, strength, and choice to retain personal sovereignty over her affairs are something to look to for inspiration. And unlike Scarlett, you are living in the twenty-first century, and therefore you have far more choices than she did.

How can you raise your vibration to a level where you can harness the power of the chakras, specifically the sacral chakra and its magnetic force that mixes love, creativity, career, sex, and finances in a way that benefits you instead of hurts you?

Scarlett's Transformation

ACT 2

Mind
I'll think about it
tomorrow.
I can do it

Heart
Obsession with Ashley
drives her, but true love
lies with Rhett.
Loves Tara

Courage
Does what's needed in spite
of how she feels. Chooses to
take control over her own
financial affairs. Ignores
society's judgment

ACT 1

ACT 3

Challenge:
Infatuated with Ashley
Wilkes
Surviving changes of Old
South. Civil War

Resolution:
Ashley, realizes she loves
Rhett too late, returns to
Tara, forges on, "I'll find a
way to get him back"

Summary

Becoming a producer, leading with sovereignty, and maintaining a balanced second chakra is all about knowing your worth, feeling good about your earnings, managing your finances well, acting with integrity, pursuing your passions and interests, creating to your heart's delight, and relating to others through romance and sensuality in a healthy, empowered, guilt-free way. Like producing a movie, you are able to make financially sound decisions. When mounting your film project, when it comes to your life, you ask, 'Will this be profitable?' before making any decisions. In other words, "Will this benefit my life in the long run or will it bring me harm?" Living your life according to the answer that comes is called wisdom.

Remember, you are the screenwriter, and just like Scarlett, no matter what life throws at you, you have the power to continually rewrite your script in a way that puts you in the role of the victor instead of the victim. Let go of your Old South, embrace your New South. You'll learn how in the next chapter, Listen to Your Director, Lead with Confidence.

Notes

STEP FOUR

Listen to Your Director

Lead with Confidence

The Wizard of Oz

DOROTHY
But, how do I start for Emerald City?

GLINDA
It's always best to start at the beginning…and
all you do is follow the yellow brick road.

DOROTHY
But…what happens if I…

GLINDA
Just follow the yellow brick road.

Dorothy looks down at her feet as she starts to
follow the yellow brick road. Glinda is o.s. The
mayor of the Munchkin City and other munchkins
give her advice.

DOROTHY
My! People come and go so quickly
here! Follow the yellow brick road.
Follow the yellow brick road?

MAYOR
Follow the yellow brick road.

FIRST MUNCHKIN
Follow the yellow brick road.

WOMAN
Follow the yellow brick road.

BARRISTER
Follow the yellow brick road.

FIDDLERS
(sing)
Follow the yellow brick road.
Follow the yellow brick road.

A Beautiful Mind

John Nash (Russell Crowe) is a mathematical genius going to graduate school at Princeton in 1948. He's a socially awkward guy who keeps mainly to himself and his roommate, Charles. After graduating and getting a job as a professor, he meets and marries Alicia (Jennifer Connelly). Meanwhile, the government involves him in breaking Soviet codes, which leads him deep into a conspiracy theory. Nash grows more and more paranoid as time goes on.

He becomes withdrawn and obsessed with the case, until it's discovered that there was no conspiracy, nor was there any government project. Both existed only in his mind. He is diagnosed with schizophrenia and institutionalized.

His act 1 challenge and biggest antagonist is mental illness. At one point he decides to go off his medication, only to wind up reverting to a paranoid state. The turning point is when Alicia is about to leave him, and he determines that neither Charles nor the little girl he sees is real—they are figments of his imagination. Alicia decides to stay by his side as he struggles to ignore them. He describes it as going on a "diet of the mind." Like being on a diet where you avoid certain foods, he chooses to ignore the voices and imaginary people, rather than go back on his medication.

In act 3, it's the 1970s. He returns to the Princeton library and his passion for math, and then eventually makes it back to teaching. In 1994 he wins the Nobel Prize for the game theory he discovered years before.

The Director's Role: Wise Guide

"A film director is a person who directs the making and the production of a film. They visualize the screenplay, controlling a film's artistic and dramatic aspects, while guiding the technical crew and actors in the fulfillment of his or her vision. In some cases, film directors do not have absolute creative control.

The screenplay includes directions for the filming of every scene, but it is the director who guides the entire project. Without a director, there is no leadership." http://en.wikipedia.org/wiki/Film_director

Listen to Your Director
Lead with Confidence

My son Jack is a junior in high school, and since he was twelve, he's wanted to be a film director. (He was definitely born to the right mother.) By the time he was old enough to hold a pencil, he would spend hours with his younger brother, Christopher, drawing and sketching. It wasn't unusual to find colored pencils in every corners of the room, and I was constantly straightening up piles of paper that they'd gone through in the course of a day.

When Jack was ten, I took the boys to Disney World. Most of the children and their parents casually looked at the Mickey Mouse exhibit showing how Mickey has transformed over time; Jack commented on the way his eyes were drawn. Instead of watching cartoons for the pure enjoyment of it, he was figuring out how they were made. He saved up his birthday money to buy his first movie camera at twelve and started making zombie films with his friends. He taught himself how to use Final Cut Express, film editing software, and how to create special effects on his computer. He's since upgraded his equipment several times. Becoming a film director is his dream.

Which is why I was upset when his first term report card wasn't just bad; he actually failed a class and was on the verge of failing another.

Now, I'm a personal coach, and I'm in the middle of writing this book, so I'm not proud of the fact

> *When you are criticized, criticizing your critic only brings you down to their level.*
>
> *—Joyce Meyers*

that instead of using my training, my first reaction was to play the part of the Wicked Witch of the West.

I completely lost it. Images of a thirty-five-year-old failure-to-launch man living in my basement crossed my mind. I could already smell the pot smoke.

But that wasn't my main fear. I was afraid for him—of him living a life of unfulfilled dreams. As a parent, it's a fine line we have to balance between telling our kids their grades matter while also letting them know that they can still be successful even without perfect scores. But the path they take toward their dream will be easier with good grades. There are exceptions, but face it, we all want our kids to do well in school.

"Listen, this is your life, not mine, and if you want to ruin it, that's your business. But let me tell you, when you guys are grown up, I'm moving on. You'll either be homeless or in college," I said, not calmly.

While I was ranting and raving, a voice in my head said, *Amy, this isn't helping.* In the past I'd tried taking away privileges like video games and television. It had a minimal impact. I tried incentives, like financial rewards. But he pointed out that none of those things work. They just make him feel worse. I'd been to the guidance counselor. The ability to learn isn't an issue. Past performance told me he simply wasn't living up to his potential.

He was defensive. He didn't like his teacher. I was never satisfied. He accused me of making his grades about me, not him. He went on to tell me that he didn't know when the teacher collected homework (yeah, right). You know the drill. He finally stormed out of the room.

About fifteen minutes later, after we both calmed down, he came back downstairs. I put on my coach crown and did my best to play wise guide. "Jack. I know you want to go to film school. I know this is important to you, so what's it going to take for you to get your grades back up so that you can do it?" I asked.

"I don't know," he said. He admitted to not doing his homework at all.

"What's preventing you from doing your work? Because you know you have the ability to get good grades. You've done it before. What's stopping you from doing what you know you need to do?" I asked.

He said, "You see, if you'd just talk to me like this!"

"Well, I'm talking to you like this now," I answered.

"All right, Mom. I'll tell you. I'm not interested in any of the subjects at school, except for maybe Ethics. I don't know why I'm like this, but my laziness knows no bounds. I will sit in my room for hours, staring at the wall, knowing that I have a paper to write, but I won't write it. I don't know why. I can't explain it. I just don't do it," he said.

He went on to add, "Nobody thinks that I can be a film director. Everybody tells me it's too hard and that I should pick something else."

Now we were getting somewhere.

Ironically, I'd already written this chapter (minus this section, obviously). I said to him, "Jack. You have a powerful inner film critic right now called Lazy Jack. Lazy Jack is telling you that you shouldn't bother trying in school or even doing anything at all, because it's pointless. You're not going to ever become a film director anyway. You have to stop listening to Lazy Jack and start listening to Director Jack," I said.

I handed him this chapter. He nodded his head and smiled as he read it. He got it.

"You want to be a film director for a reason, and you have to explore why that is. You may find something else on your path to becoming a director that interests you more, but you're meant to go in that direction. I'm not good at playing the part of Tiger Mom, but I guess that's what I'm going to have to do. Be prepared, because I'm going to be kicking your ass from here to film school. You're not going to like it, but you're going to film school, and you are going to look back on this time some day and thank me," I said.

Man, what parent hasn't said that, right?

I did a good job making a home where my kids felt free to create, but Jack's grades told me he needed more structure, and sometimes I needed to be an antagonist in his life story. But most of the time, I strive to be his supporting player.

It hasn't been easy. He still pushes back. He's annoyed when I make him show me his planner and all of his homework. It's up to him, not me, to do what he needs to do. He's bored with the subjects, and it makes it hard for him to focus, but I keep reminding him to listen to Director Jack.

This choice we have—to listen to the inner critic or the inner director—is much like the choice I had to be the good witch or the bad witch. And it's like this in business, isn't it? I can reflect upon my experience managing teams. My staff always performed at their best when I coached them, not when I imposed rules or the company made restrictive policies. Everyone's on their own path, and if you can help them to identify and remove their own roadblocks to success, there's no need for rewards or punishments. (Well, maybe rewards. Rewards are always nice.)

We all have a Lazy Jack. I have a Lazy Amy who hates paperwork. This was a good lesson for me, too. I continue to remind Jack to listen to his inner film director. For him, it's a literal director, but we all have an inner film director, and it's our director who will get us going in the right direction, following our own version of the yellow brick road.

This step is about controlling your thoughts, or going on a diet of the mind. You will tap into the voice of your inner film director, your wise intuitive guide, for guidance and to build self-confidence, as opposed to the voice of the inner film critic, who wants to keep you stuck in your act 1 challenge.

Your Inner Film Critic

The voice of your inner film critic tends to be the voice you hear more than anything when you're stuck. It's the voice of fear and self-doubt. While it isn't a voice of schizophrenia, as it was in Nash's case, it's still a voice that will hold you back to live in an unreal state. It's the voice that tells you not to—one that reminds you of past failures. It tells you things it thinks will protect you from harm. It's the voice that says you're not enough...not smart enough, not thin enough, not rich enough, or not educated enough. It tells you that you don't have enough credentials. *It's never going to happen for you. You don't have enough money. You're too old. You're too young.* It's the voice of self-doubt.

Why do you have this inner critic if it holds you back? What good is it? In some ways, it's protective. There are times when it's wise to hold back, do more research, or proceed with caution, but it can also be a fight or flight response to stress that kicks in when it isn't necessary. It confuses your desire to venture into the unknown with entering a war zone. You may have heard it referred to as the Monkey Mind or Lizard Brain. Your inner film critic tries to protect you from danger, humiliation, or failure, so when you're about to do something new, or leave something that's no longer working, the inner film critic is there to caution you about what's "out there." But the problem is that you tend to give it a little more weight than it deserves. Not only that, but your inner film critic loves to gather evidence to prove her point. If it's credentials she says you lack, she'll list all the people who are more educated, experienced, or talented than you are. If you want to write a book, she'll jump in to persuade you not to waste your time on something you've never done before. You could fail, it could flop, it will be a total waste of time, and you'll only end up making a complete fool of yourself. *Stick to what you're good at*, she'll say. Ask her what you're good at, and she won't have much of a response. She doesn't think you're good at much of anything, except for maybe cleaning toilets, and even then, judging by the ever-so-subtle ring clinging to the sides of the bowl, you could still improve.

She'll point to scientific articles that say women your age are destined to be dumpy because of things like hormones and slowed metabolisms, and she'll remind you that all the women in your family who are overweight. Aunt Betty, the bombshell who maintained her girlish figure well into her seventies, will be called out as an anomaly. Any fit women your age must have better genes or money to hire a personal trainer. Not only that, but the notion that you may be lovable just as you are is scoffed at. You have to be perfect. You can't be perfect, but you have to be perfect; therefore you can never win. Not only can't you improve, but you can't love yourself either.

Haven't found your ideal relationship yet? Your inner film critic will tell you it's because you're too fat, too old, or not rich enough. She'll remind you of all the women out there who are better than you, women any guy you take an interest in is bound to discover after a while...*so don't get too comfy*.

Get a new job? Start a new business? *Fagetaboutit!*

I call my inner film critic Pia, short for Pain in the Ass. Pia speaks in a thick Boston accent and uses a lot of hand gestures. She also smokes a lot, wears too much hot-pink lipstick that bleeds out the edges of her mouth, and we won't even discuss the clumpy mascara. It isn't pretty. I'm fairly certain she's also an alcoholic.

Your inner film critic doesn't always know what she's talking about, and she can keep you stuck if you listen to her, when you know on a deeper level that you need to move forward. Not everything in life is worthy of stage fright.

Your Inner Film Director

How do you conquer the voice of your inner film critic? You tap into the voice of your inner film director instead. Your inner director is your truth, your inner wisdom encouraging you to take the next step. It shows up as a thought, an inner urging, or a calling to do something new or leave something old. It was your inner film director who guided you to purchase this book. The inner critic is going to try to keep you stuck in the past—the world that's known, but your inner film director will guide you to take that next step into the world of the unknown—to take a risk.

I like to think of my director as my inner Glinda, the Good Witch of the North. When you tune into this wise source for guidance, you find your true north. Since everything in Oz is a manifestation of Dorothy's subconscious mind, you have to see Glinda as her inner wisdom, her director. She doesn't tell Dorothy how to go home, but she does point her in the direction she should go to find her answers. She gives Dorothy her power by placing the ruby slippers on her feet. She doesn't tell her to stay where she is, but to trust—*just follow the yellow brick road.*

When Dorothy and her friends fall asleep in a field of poppies, right before they're about to reach the Emerald City, it's a metaphor for those times in life when you're just about to reach your dream goal and something tells you, *Retreat! Give up! Don't go there! You don't know what's going to happen! Stop now, while there's still time to go to back to where you came from!*

In the movie it's a wicked witch who casts a spell upon Dorothy and her friends. And that's just like your inner film critic—when you listen to her, it's as if you're under a spell. Getting back to our horror film analogy, it's akin to a haunting. Like the ghosts who cling to their earthly life, trapped in a dimension between this one and the next, your inner film critic is going to keep you in limbo. You will suffer as you struggle in an in-between state. You'll try to shut out your inner wisdom—which will not be silenced and can't help but urge you to "see the light"—as your inner critic remains trapped in the past, which is dead and gone. Like John Nash, when he shut out the imaginary people and voices who made him fearful and paranoid, you need to exorcise your negative inner voice.

It's Glinda, the Good Witch of the North, who breaks the spell that revives Dorothy and her friends. Your inner Glinda will awaken you to the truth. You may think of your inner film director as your inner wisdom, your intuitive source, angels, God, Jesus, your higher power, the universe, source, or your spirit. It's your true essence, saying to you: *You are meant for more. If you listen to me, I will guide you down the path to your dream.*

Your inner film director will also tell you when you are headed in the wrong direction. You will know she's talking and not your inner film critic because of the way you feel when you imagine taking the next step. How does it feel in your gut? Is it exciting? Does it feel right? It's sometimes difficult to distinguish between fear keeping you from forging ahead and a knowing that what you're about to do isn't right. Something I've learned quite recently is to determine whether or not what

I'm contemplating is my goal or someone else's. Your family, friends, and even society have ideas for how you should live your life. The trick is to determine what is right for you.

Have I mastered this step? No, I haven't. In fact I haven't mastered any of them. One of the things my own inner film critic has said to me as I'm writing this book is this: *Your life isn't perfect, so who are you to teach this? You're not in a relationship. Your finances aren't in the best shape. You could still stand to lose a few pounds. Don't you think you should get all of that in order before you do this work?*

The standard of success in the field of self-help book writing is to have achieved millionaire status, have the perfect spouse, and to look amazing all at once. This is ridiculous. No one has a perfect life. I'm reminded of one of the principles of yoga, Buddhism, and Christianity: non-judgment. To practice non-judgment is to honor the divinity in everyone, and to understand that no one in this life has achieved perfection. I strive to observe and accept people wherever they are, including me. Choose to love yourself rather than be critical and judgmental of who you are and where you are at the moment. Forgive your mistakes. Believe me; I can be incredibly hard on myself. I've heard all the inner voices of doubt and not enough that I've described in this chapter. None of us will ever arrive at that ideal place, because that's not what life is. That's what death is. I loved reading that in Esther and Jerry Hicks' book *Manifest Your Desires*. As I've studied principles of the law of attraction, I've often felt tremendous pressure or shame around not having manifested everything I want, because according to the law, it means I'm not attracting it. But this is absurd. As the Hickses said, achieving it all is to be dead. We can only work towards that place, and through acceptance and non-judgment, enjoy the process and the path. Much like going on a road trip, part of the joy is in the journey, not just the destination. Along the path, we often change our mind about what we want, or we may make adjustments.

My inner director reminded me that I am simply the spiritual teacher—the conduit of information. I am the eternal student of life. I am the messenger, and to listen to the negativity of my inner critic is to shoot the messenger—in this case, to commit creative suicide. I would get nothing done if I filtered every thought or idea through the judgment of my perfectionistic inner film critic. Remember this in any of your own endeavors. No matter what, there is always more to learn.

The Third Chakra: Solar Plexus

Your third chakra is located in the area of the solar plexus, and it corresponds to your stomach, abdomen, upper intestines, liver, gall bladder, kidney, pancreas, adrenal glands, spleen, and middle spine. Its color is Yellow. Its element is fire. Its demon is *shame*.

The mental and emotional issues of this chakra have to do with trust, self-esteem, self-confidence, self-respect, decision making, personal honor, and your ability to hear constructive feedback. Any difficulties in this area have to do with maintaining personal power. It's the part of your development related to the ego, and it is where you develop your intuition—your gut instincts.

"How about a little fire, scarecrow?" said the witch.

This step is about the mind and what you think about. While the energetic connection hits you in your solar plexus, it begins in the brain.

"If I only had a brain," sang the scarecrow.

The element of this chakra is fire. Interesting that a tactic the witch uses to attack her is flames. Dorothy finds her courage, develops an incredible amount of self-confidence, shuts out the voice of her inner film critic, and when faced with her villain at the end, doesn't hesitate to stand up to her wicked ways. Dorothy douses the flame with a bucket of water, and the witch melts into nothingness. Dorothy's goal of killing the witch (destroying her inner film critic and its voice of self-doubt, fear, and inadequacy), and returning to the wizard with her broomstick, are powerful motivators. She refuses to remain stuck in Oz. Her vision of returning home to Kansas is greater than her fears.

In *The Wizard of Oz*, the brick road is yellow, the color of the third chakra, which is symbolic of the self-confidence required of Dorothy to make the journey.

When you think about it, the ability to take a stand for your life and say with confidence, *I deserve to have great friends, to live in a nurturing, supportive environment, and to love my work* takes high self-esteem. The ability to listen to your intuition and to stand up to your wicked witch takes courage—*guts*.

Having the guts to do something and trusting your gut instincts is what this chakra is about. This is the area where you are challenged to believe in yourself first, to be authentic, and to have confidence enough to move forward along the path down which you can feel your inner director guiding you. Like Scarlett O'Hara, you "think about that tomorrow" and keep pushing that critical voice off to a day that doesn't come. Like John Nash, you go on a diet of the mind and shut out the voice of the inner film critic. Just for today, do what needs to be done. Like Jack, ignore the voice that wants you to do nothing.

Your intuition speaks to you through your body. Stomach upset, gas, bloating, emotional eating, and eating disorders may be signs that you are not honoring the self and living with high self-esteem. It may tell you to avoid certain situations or people who are not good for you, such as significant others who, instead of cheering you on, tell you your ideas are stupid, silly nonsense. It may signal a time to leave a job or to pursue a different career or something creative that, at that moment, seems nonsensical.

Problems with your third chakra can manifest themselves as intestinal, stomach, and other digestive disorders. This could be the result of ignoring your intuition for an extended period of time. You literally "swallow" it instead of acknowledging it, and it eats away at you, little by little, begging to be heard. And it's relentless. It won't give up on you, even if your internal organs buckle under the pressure.

Before I started *Star in Your Own Life Story, LLC*, I worked in an office where some of my colleagues would keep bowls of M&Ms. Throughout the day I'd find myself grabbing a handful. And I was eating a little too much at lunch. Eventually, I gained fifteen pounds. I wasn't listening to my inner director. She was telling me it was time to start my own business, but I had doubts and felt under-confident. Pia was there, pouring herself a stiff drink. She'd light her cigarette, take a drag, blow smoke into the air, and say, *Who are you to be a professional author? Yeah, you wrote a book and it won four awards, but that doesn't mean you're any good! You, a speaker? Huh! Who do you think you are? You're kidding yourself. You'll never be that good. You're a fraud, and people are going to find out you don't know what you're doing. You're going to fail if you even attempt it. Stay here where it's safe and you know a check is coming every two weeks. Don't be so irresponsible, so selfish. You have two kids to think about. You don't even have an area of expertise! Get a grip on yourself. Better yet, eat some M&Ms instead. It'll make you forget your dreams.*

When I became Reiki I certified and one of my fellow students practiced on me, she said that she could intuitively feel an imbalance in that area of my body. As she placed her hands over my abdomen for five minutes, I experienced a beam of light extending up and out from me. I mentioned in step one that my feet often bother me when my instincts tell me there is something I'm supposed to be doing, but I hold back. My stomach is another way my body speaks to me. My solar plexus chakra, the energetic connection between my thoughts and feelings and my physical body, spoke to me on an intuitive level. My gut literally told me to write and to stop letting my self-doubt get in the way.

Yeah, that's right, Pia. Now clean up your act and find someone else to pick on.

My inner Glinda was right there all along with her encouragement and support, and to guide me down the path laid out before me. I just needed to pay more attention to her than to Pia. (Pia's a little messed up.)

Shame is a powerful motivation that erodes self-esteem, so an environment of shaming can lead to an imbalanced solar plexus. Keep in mind that your life's antagonists are often outward manifestations of your inner film critic, so if you listen to your inner critic's messages—that you ought to be ashamed of yourself for liking something others may find unusual, for example—you may be attracting a person or situation that will confirm your inner critic by criticizing your choices.

A person who experiences a deficiency in the solar plexus can have health issues in the areas mentioned. They may have low energy, be quiet, withdrawn, and stuck—unable to move forward. They may choose to stimulate their energy with caffeine or have addictions. They go through life on the shadow side of their victim archetype. A person can also overcompensate by having a massive ego, which is really just masking their low self-esteem. They can be manipulative, aggressive, or controlling. They can't relax. When you view the scene from *Defending Your Life* in your Star Pack, "I'm on Trial for Being Afraid?" you'll hear

Bob Diamond (Rip Torn) say to Daniel, "You feel it in your stomach, right?" Fears and self-doubts go hand-in-hand.

One way to overcome the inner film critic and problems in the third chakra is to build up your self-confidence by listening to the voice of your inner film director.

Ways to tap into your inner film director

Meditation doesn't have to mean sitting on a cushion with your back straight and incense burning. You don't have to give up meat, wear Birkenstocks, or go to a sweat lodge. I sit in my recliner, play some relaxing music, and close my eyes for twenty minutes. I find my writing flows better when I'm able to just sit and breathe and quiet my mind. My inner wisdom speaks to me in that state. Relaxing, taking a walk, writing in a journal, getting a massage, taking a hot bath, doing something that allows you to sit still and *be* gives your mind a rest and allows you to access your source of wisdom. Be aware of your dreams. Powerful messages can come through your dreams, so keep a dream journal beside your bed and write them down before they leave your consciousness.

Another way to tap into the voice of your inner film director is to notice words and voices that come to you. It can come from within but also from people. When I was ready to move on from my job with the Department of Environmental Protection, a friend of mine asked me, "Have you ever thought of just getting a new job?"

My job had become boring and my commute had been taking as much as two hours due to road construction. I was exhausted and uninspired. I took some time to write down all the things I loved to do—my skills, education, experience, hobbies. That job was draining me physically. Something needed to give. When I made the mental shift—the decision to look for a new job, I received a call the next day from a consultant at Brainshark. I was working there just a few weeks later. I believe that when you make a decision to honor a thought that it's time to do something else, and you spend time thinking about what you really, really want, you attract, on an energetic level, what it is that you feel. I'm not at all surprised anymore when people call me just as I thought of them. It happened to me just yesterday.

"We don't realize that, somewhere within us all, there does exist a supreme self who is eternally at peace."

—Elizabeth Gilbert
Eat, Pray, Love

I was thinking about how nice it would be to have plans Friday night, and a friend called and invited me to a cocktail party. I received some disappointing news the other day, which caused my inner film critic to kick into high gear. Yesterday, I awoke to a song playing on the radio, *Girl on Fire* by Alicia Keys. The lyrics lifted me up and kept me in a happy frame of mind for the rest of the day. This morning my alarm went off to Rihanna singing *Shine Like a Diamond*. I had been lying in bed thinking that perhaps I wasn't meant to shine as a professional author and speaker. This is what I mean about your inner film director. I tuned in to her station—in this case, a literal radio station. And that's what you need to do to shut out your inner film critic. Change the station to the one playing uplifting music and who will fill you with warm, comforting, encouraging thoughts.

Your inner director speaks to you through a sense of inner knowing. You can't explain it. You just *know*—like knowing that "he's the one" or "this is my house" or "yes, I'm ready to move on from this job." Look for signs. Books that pertain to what you're thinking about will fall off the shelf, or your eyes will naturally gravitate to the correct title.

Be in your body, and notice if you are experiencing any issues in your digestive system. My stomach kicks in whenever I'm around someone who's not good for me. It will often pick up on a person's energy before I consciously realize that a person isn't right. Like getting butterflies before you're about to give a speech or go on stage, you'll get nervous knots in your stomach as a warning, too. Emotional eating is another sign that you're nervous, feeling ashamed, or under-confident.

Nash's "diet of the mind" is such a great metaphor for ignoring the voice of your inner film critic as though it were the voice of schizophrenia. Listening to your inner film critic can keep you stuck in fear and what-if thinking. *What if it doesn't work? What if I fail? What if I lose everything? What if I completely mess up my life?* Diet of the mind is what this step is all about. It's about cutting out or lessening the voice of the inner film critic so that you can hear the voice of truth, the voice of your inner director. Tune in to your solar plexus chakra, your digestion, and notice how it feels in your body as you contemplate a decision to move ahead with something. Does it give you feelings of inner peace and self-confidence? Tune in to your core, listen to your gut, and trust your source before making a decision. Like Dorothy, you are believing in the beauty and goodness of your inner self—your inner Glinda.

In *A Beautiful Mind*, John Nash finds the courage to battle schizophrenia with the loving support of his wife. She plays a major role in his ability to confront his mental illness and the fears the voices instill in him. This movie is all about the mind and the power of thoughts. He recognizes that he has this incredibly destructive inner voice that tells him things that aren't real. He chooses not to listen to it. In the end, he delivers a beautiful acceptance speech, showing how much he connected to his heart. The movie clip is in your Star Pack.

John Nash's Transformation

ACT 2

Mind
Diet of the mind.
Shuts out voices/things
that aren't real

Courage
Deal with Schizophrenia

Heart
"The only real thing is
love."

ACT 1

ACT 3

Challenge:
Mental Illness

Resolution:
Leads "normal" life. Wins
Nobel Prize

Jim's Story

Jim came to me feeling completely burned out. He'd been working as an engineer for about fifteen years; since he got out of college, but he'd discovered another passion—healing. He was just six months away from graduating from massage therapy school, and he was already a Reiki master. Trying to be a full-time engineer and part-time healer took up nearly all of his time, and he knew there was no way he could continue doing both. He wanted to be a full-time healer but didn't see how it was possible, because he made little to nothing. He relied on his engineering job to pay his bills. To Jim, his choices were to either starve as a happy healer or to live with abundance as an unhappy engineer. He was beginning to resent his day job, but there was no way he could quit.

The people who came to see Jim usually had health issues, so he felt guilty asking them for money. As a result, he did the work for free, bartered with them, or charged them so little it was insignificant. Jim's engineering work was very impersonal. His company gave him a paycheck, so he never had to deal with the business of determining prices and asking for payment. The fact that he was approaching his healing work as a hobby was out of sync with his desire to earn a living at it.

Jim said that he believed it was spiritually wrong to charge people for his services. But the truth was that Jim was afraid people wouldn't hire him if he charged them anything. His attitude was masking his insecurity about his value as a healer. What it really came down to was a fear of rejection. He was so afraid that his talents would be wasted and his business would fail, that he charged little to nothing as a way to ensure people continually sought him out. On the one hand, he knew he was a gifted healer, but on the other, he had absolutely no confidence in his ability to succeed. Interestingly, he attracted non-paying clients with the same mentality, i.e., "I doubt this will work, but I have nothing to lose because I haven't invested anything."

Healing was something he'd grown to love, and the idea that it wouldn't work out was too much to imagine. Through our work together, he realized that by not charging for his time, he was teaching people not to value his services or to value their care. He was basically telling them his work had no value, therefore it was free, and moreover, he actually expected people to think he was a better person for it! Meanwhile, the guy down the street, trained to do the same work, was attracting more new business and making good money, because people perceived him to do better work, i.e., *He must be good if he charges so much.* He was attracting people who believed in their capacity to get well and who were willing to invest their time and money in their own treatment.

Jim rationalized that his problem was his day job. What he was really doing was using it as an excuse. He hid behind his desire to serve as a way to avoid something that made him feel uncomfortable. What he was beginning to learn was that although his job felt like an antagonistic force in his life, what it was teaching him to do was value his time and his talents.

Jim determined a fair price for his services, printed up a brochure, and rather than indulging his fear, mustered up the courage to present his pricing structure to prospective clients just as the local barber, dry cleaner, or restaurant would. He also began to view his day job as a gift, because it paid the bills while he started his side business. But this was just the first stage of his change. He'd just entered the second act of his movie. His act 1 conflict was being overwhelmed trying to do everything, but as we moved into act 2, what began to reveal itself was the fact that he was afraid that he'd fail at doing something he knew he was going to love, and then he'd really be stuck. So, in a way, his behavior was a self-fulfilling prophesy. He was virtually guaranteeing failure by undervaluing his services. For Jim, his inner film critic gave him the constant message that "real" healers are able to work for free because they are so spiritual that money is unimportant. His inner director ensured him that he was a talented healer with a lot to offer, and he deserved to be compensated well for his time.

When I asked him, "Do you really believe people shouldn't be paid for their services?" Jim had to say, "No."

In fact he felt that people in the field of alternative therapies were undervalued. He also admitted that he was extremely good at what he did.

Even though he put together his pricing, it didn't mean he

completely changed his thinking around it. He still had guilt. He still had self-doubt. He still feared no one would pay him for his time, or worse, they would ask for their money back. But Jim made the decision to charge for his time in spite of his fears. He chose to shut out the disempowering, negative internal dialogue, and then began employing a strategy to get his mind in alignment with his thoughts. He chose to step outside his comfort zone and stand up to his fear.

And that's the interesting thing. Jim's thoughts around charging for his work resulted in no financial gain. But changing his thoughts required him to first change his behavior. Nothing brings about change faster than taking action.

Jim also realized that he didn't want to leave his engineering work. He still enjoyed it. He wanted an eclectic career where he made a living combing both of his talents, but he wanted to do it in a more balanced way. Over time, his fees became a natural part of the work he was doing. By charging a fair price, he was also able to place limits around the number of clients he took on, thus reducing his feeling of overwhelm.

Summary

The voice of your inner film critic is the voice of self-doubt, low self-esteem, and "not enough." Listening to this voice will cause you to be under-confident and to remain stuck in what-if, fear-based thinking. It will prevent you from achieving your goals, whether it's going after a promotion at work, starting your own business, attracting and maintaining a healthy relationship, achieving weight or fitness goals, finishing your book, or any other vision you have for your life. It will try to convince you that your desire for a simpler life is really you just being a quitter. Self-confidence is probably one of the most important qualities you can ever develop, and it comes from listening to your inner wisdom.

To move forward and to maintain a healthy third chakra, learn to tap into and trust the voice of your inner film director. Your inner film director is your wise inner guide. You may think of this voice as the voice of inner wisdom, your higher power, universe, source, God, intuition, or angels speaking to you. Glinda, the Good Witch of the North, guided Dorothy down her yellow brick road. She didn't tell Dorothy how to get home but showed her the first step, and then the next. Dorothy trusted Glinda; in other words, she trusted her intuition. Glinda, the Good Witch of the North, helps Dorothy to find her "true north."

Repeat the voice of your inner film director as a way to train your mind. Go on a diet of the mind to shut out the voice of your inner film critic. Your thoughts create your reality. Spend time every day feeding your mind healthy, empowering, visionary thoughts, so that you can find your way home to your true self.

Notes

Notes

STEP FIVE

Be the Star

Lead with Love

The Holiday

Arthur Abbot

Iris, in the movies we have leading ladies
and we have the best friend. You, I can tell,
are a leading lady, but for some reason
you are behaving like the best friend.

Iris

You're so right. You're supposed to be
the leading lady of your own life, for
god's sake! Arthur, I've been going to a
therapist for three years, and she's never
explained anything to me that well. That
was brilliant. Brutal, but brilliant.

The Holiday

The 2006 movie The Holiday is an endearing romantic comedy with co-protagonists. Iris (Kate Winslet) and Amanda (Cameron Diaz), swap houses for three weeks over the Christmas holiday. Each of them decide spur-of-the-moment to vacate their lives when Kate finds out that the man she's been in love with for three years is engaged, and Amanda discovers that her boyfriend has been sleeping with his receptionist.

When Iris arrives in LA, she enters Amanda's world of luxury. As the owner of her own advertising agency that specializes in movie trailers, Amanda's done quite well. Iris's quaint stone cottage forty minutes outside of London is just what the doctor ordered for Amanda.

Iris befriends one of Amanda's neighbors, the elderly but charming Arthur Abbott, a retired screenwriter. Over dinner, Iris confides in Arthur that she's in LA to get over Jasper, a writer who has been selfishly dangling a carrot in front of her for years. In what sounded like a somewhat brief affair that ended three years before, she found out he'd been two-timing her with a woman who worked for the same newspaper. Instead of telling him to buzz off, she maintains a friendship with him and lives with the grief of loving someone who takes advantage of her. Jasper even phones her from halfway around the world to disrupt her vacation and ask her to read a chapter from his new book. As always, she agrees.

Over dinner, Arthur points out that she is clearly a leading lady, but she behaves more like the best friend. He recommends she watch a variety of old movies. Iris suspects his recommendation list is intentional, since they each have strong leading ladies "with gumption."

Back in Surrey, Amanda is disrupted in the middle of the night by Iris's brother, Graham (Jude Law), knocking on her door. This is their "meet cute," the term Arthur uses to describe two people who meet and wind up falling in love. She's already decided that the trip was a mistake and plans to return home the next day. In a moment completely out of character for Amanda, she decides to have sex with Graham. She rationalizes that because she's on vacation and leaving, they will never see one another again. But of course, she doesn't, and they do.

Iris meets Miles (Jack Black) in their "meet cute" when he shows up looking for Amanda's ex-boyfriend. The Santa Ana winds blow sand into Iris's eye, which Miles kindly offers to remove.

Iris and Miles become friends, and when Miles finds out his girlfriend, an actress, has been cheating on him, they discover they have something in common—both know the pain of unrequited love. By the third act, the two of them have grown fond of one another, but Jasper shows up at Iris's door to continue with his selfish game. This time, Iris learns the lesson, finds her "gumption" like the movie heroines in Arthur's films, and in her leading-lady moment, kicks him to the curb. When Miles's girlfriend tries to get him to take her back, he also finds his courage to say no.

Meanwhile, back in Surrey, Amanda and Graham continue to see each other. Amanda confides in him that she hasn't been able to cry since her father left when she was fifteen. Her parent's divorce had broken her heart; she'd sobbed for weeks, but then decided she needed to be strong. From then on, Amanda's pattern when it comes to men is to push them away, which is what she tries to do with Graham several times.

It turns out that Graham is a widower with two young daughters, a fact that he concealed from Amanda, confessing that he doesn't know how to mix being a full-time father with the dating world. The two try to figure out a way to continue their romance while being realistic about the prospects of success, given their extremely long-distance romance. On her way to the airport, she is finally able to let go of her always-be-strong demeanor and cries over the prospect of losing him. Her ability to cry is a sign from her inner director that she can't let this one go. In her leading-lady moment, she asks the cab driver to turn around and she runs back to Graham.

In the end, the four of them, along with Graham's daughters, ring in the New Year together.

The Four Roles

- **Extra**—The nonspeaking role. Serves as backdrop to main character
- **Supporting Player**—The best friend. There to support the main character
- **Antagonist**—The villain. Mirrors lead character's inner film critic. Lead character's teacher. Challenge to overcome
- **Star**—The protagonist, aka leading lady or man, hero or heroine. Makes the journey. Learns the lessons. Experiences the transformation. Inspires the audience

Be the Star
Lead with Love

We are all protagonists in our life story. But have you ever felt insignificant, like a movie extra—mere scenery in someone else's life? I'm sure you play a supporting role, whether it's at work or at home, but has it ever cost you your self-esteem? Like Iris in the opening scene to this chapter, have you ever felt as if you were always the best friend, never the leading lady? How about that antagonist—are you your own worst enemy, or have you ever antagonized someone else?

This chapter will teach you how to step fully into your leading role as the star in your own life story, in other words, to step into your archetypal role as the heroine.

Imagine for a moment that you're sitting in a movie theater as a member of the audience. There are ten actors in this scene. You have your lead character and several supporting players—the central character's friends, colleagues, and family members. Total strangers serve as backdrops. There's an antagonist, and there are extras without speaking parts.

If this was a scene from your love life, who would be in the lead role, the supporting roles, and the extras? Who or what would be your antagonist?

If this was a scene from your work life, who would be in each role?

How about your creative life?

What about when it comes to your health, fitness, or your self-image?

And your home?

Life requires you to play all roles in various circumstances. But when it comes to your ability to achieve the life you desire, you need to be a star. You need to take the lead. How do you feel about that? What thoughts or emotions does that evoke in you?

Extra

Let's talk about being the extra for a moment. If your life were a movie, you'd be an extra whenever you sat among a crowd at a football game or commuted to work on the train. There are times when you want to serve as an extra while someone else takes the lead.

But do you ever feel like a movie extra in your own life story? Do you ever feel invisible in your relationships, go unnoticed at work, or fail to put yourself first in order to maintain your own health and fitness?

Do you sit silently in meetings for fear that if you shared your idea or disagreed with your boss, you'd be humiliated, scolded, laughed at, or fired?

Do you keep your mouth shut and swallow your feelings to keep peace in a relationship, because you are afraid of what would happen if you spoke up or defended yourself? Have you ever had a friend who every so often blindsides you with an embarrassing comment, only to stay silent and say nothing?

If you have children, do you ever get so overwhelmed with caring for them that you feel like your goals have taken a backseat, until you don't even know what they are anymore?

Do you set aside time for a creative project that's been on your mind, or do you constantly put it last on your list, if it's even on your list at all?

We all have these human bodies that require proper maintenance through regular exercise and a nutrient-rich diet, but do you find yourself neglecting your own health? Are you a fast-food junkie, chocoholic, or couch potato? It's okay to indulge once in a while, but not as a way of life.

How often do you move your body? A body that isn't cared for is a body that winds up needing a lot of care, not to mention what it does to your everyday life. I once met a man whose ex-wife had become so obese that when her parents offered to take her and their two children to Hawaii, she couldn't go because she couldn't fit on the plane. This is so sad! So many people live their lives disconnected from their bodies. We are not heads walking around. We are full, complete, human beings, head to toe.

I happen to love all sorts of movement—dancing, walking, and even working out (at least when I'm done). While yoga isn't for everybody, one of the things I love about it is that it's all about bringing together mind, body, and spirit. The word yoga means "yoke" or to join. I was first introduced to yoga when my children were babies and I had just completed a program to deal with anxiety. The class was on the beach, and from the first time I tried it, I was hooked. Having spent many years working in the fitness industry as an instructor, I couldn't see the benefit of yoga. I thought it was too easy to have any effect, not to mention it seemed a bit weird. Boy was I wrong! Not only is it challenging, especially certain styles, but by slowing down your movements and being completely in your body for sixty to ninety minutes, you become reconnected. It's how I became introduced to the chakra system, as yoga helps to keep your energetic anatomy in harmony and balance and to work out issues in your chakras.

In my opinion, the best form of exercise you can do is the one you enjoy the most, because that's the one you'll stick with. Don't let anybody talk you into doing yoga, spinning, or running just because they think it's the best. Do what you love and fitness will follow.

Okay – I got a little off track there. I was talking about being a movie extra—neglecting yourself, taking a back seat in someone else's story, sitting quietly and not sticking up for yourself at work, playing a non-speaking role. Let's decide not to do that, shall we?

Supporting Player

Movies are full of great supporting players. As a mother, author, and coach, I play a supporting role. If you are a good spouse, partner, parent, and friend, you are supportive. You provide words of encouragement, tell your loved ones to go after their dreams, listen to them when they're down, build them back up, and care for them when they're sick. Dorothy had three great supporting players. John Nash had his wife, Alicia. Iris found Arthur Abbot. Professional athletes, executives, and entrepreneurs have coaches. Lots of people can play supporting roles in your life, like a parent, friend, coach, or teacher. In step seven, *Find Your Supporting Players*, you'll work on building your team.

There's nothing wrong with being a supporting player, except for when it comes at the expense of your own life. If you are so supportive of someone else that you neglect yourself—or ignore the signs that tell you this person, even a person you may love, is harming you, even if it isn't intentional on their part—then you're not starring in your own life story. You're playing the martyr, hoping through all of your self-sacrifice, you'll find the appreciation you "deserve" and somehow life will reward you for it. If you choose to stay in a relationship with a person who won't let you shine or who takes advantage of your support, like Jasper does of Iris in *The Holiday*, or your paths aren't in alignment, you are acting more like the best friend than the leading lady/man.

You can be both a star and a supportive partner. If you don't support your loved ones, you're not much of a leading character, but it can't be to the detriment of yourself. I can be a star coach, taking the lead in my role as wise, supportive director at the same time. If you are a parent, you can be both the lead in your own life and the supportive caregiver. You can still take care of your body and mind, learn new things, go out and have a good time, and pursue your goals too, even if the progress is slowed a bit. A good manager isn't only a leader, but a supportive coach who guides her team, answers questions, and acts as an advocate. When you take a leadership role in your own life, you set a great example for your loved ones. You command respect. You set an example of how you can love others and still love yourself, too.

Antagonist

Isn't it strange to think that you can actually play the part of an antagonist in another person's story? Sometimes you are the antagonist, not necessarily because you want to make someone else's life miserable, but because something about you brings out the worst in them.

Take jealousy, for example. Have you been on the receiving end of another person's jealousy? I have, and it's a terrible feeling. We've all been jealous, but it's an awful thing when someone else can't control it in themselves and they lash out at you, seemingly unaware of the fact that envy is their problem, not you. Your very being serves as an antagonistic force in their life, and the nicer you are, the worse it is for them, because now, whatever it is about you that they envy, becomes worse because you're a good person, to boot.

And ironically, that person, in turn, can become your antagonist because of the way they treat you.

To Snow White's wicked queen, Snow White was the villain who stole her limelight. In the queen's mind, Snow White was the antagonist. Same goes for Cinderella. Her stepmother and stepsisters viewed her as the biggest obstacle to their ability to succeed in life. As long as Cinderella was around, there was someone who was more beautiful, more charming, and more desirable. Dorothy's antagonist was Almira Gulch, the "wicked old witch" who tried to have Toto put down. In Oz, she actually becomes a literal witch, an outward manifestation of Gulch, and the person who provides Dorothy the opportunity to learn to stand in her power. But if you look at Dorothy from the witch's perspective, Dorothy is *her* antagonist. She has her sister's shoes. She has the power the witch craves.

You can be an antagonist in someone else's life story for no reason other than you have something that they want, whether it's a little dog, a great pair of shoes, intelligence, success, beauty, money, happiness, a healthy relationship, or security. If that's the case, then you have been brought into this person's spiritual experience as their teacher. They've been called upon to learn how to appreciate their own beauty, intelligence, and inner strength. How cool is that? I wouldn't go telling them this. They won't appreciate it, but it will make you feel a heck of a lot better knowing *it's not you.* Let them learn their life lessons on their own and back away.

If you've ever been confused by a person's antagonistic behavior toward you, look at them archetypically. What do you have that they may want? What shadow archetypes are they acting out? Perhaps you've encountered a wicked queen, vampire, or a player. The player archetype is the man or woman who treats romance as a game; the objects of their affections mere playing pieces on the giant chess board of life. Every move is strategic and designed to keep up the thrill of the con. It may confuse you to think of a particular person as your antagonist, especially if you love them, but make no mistake. If they are causing you grief, they are an antagonistic force in your life. The challenge is in seeing them realistically. Keep in mind that Dracula was incredibly charming. Not all villains appear evil. The devil usually comes in disguise. Like every great story's villain, there is an opportunity in this situation. Keep in mind that I'm speaking metaphorically. This person doesn't get up every morning and think about how they may contribute to your spiritual development, but if you are able to look at them that way, you will learn the lesson. You will feel absolutely amazing when you stop trying to change their character or put up with the situation, and you decide to edit them from your story instead, just as Iris finally does with Jasper, her antagonist in *The Holiday*, or Nash does with Charles and the government agents he sees in his mind.

If you have ever managed people, I can practically guarantee you that you served as someone's antagonist at one point or another. While you want your staff to like you and love their jobs, and you want to create an atmosphere of teamwork, there are times when you also have to establish rules, create new processes that people may not like, and discipline people for poor performance. Your staff may feel you're causing them great discomfort.

And how about parenting? I'm quite certain my two teenage

> *"I'm interested in encouraging people to be the protagonist in their own lives, It doesn't have to mean standing up against the death penalty...But just those little moments, a step toward leading an authentic life."*
>
> —*Susan Sarandon*

sons look at me as the villain from time to time, because I make them clean up after themselves and do their homework. At times, they need me to play the antagonist.

The antagonist in a story serves as the central character's greatest teacher. Growth is a result of a challenge, problem, or situation that calls upon you to learn new things, tap into your intuition, find your voice, become more assertive, and stand in your power. While you naturally want everything in your life to go smoothly and be all wine and roses, true spiritual growth and transformation comes by surmounting difficulty. It's all in how you view it.

That's what it means to be an antagonist in someone else's story, but what about those times when you are the antagonist in your own?

Let's say you are playing the lead in a movie, and your character's challenge is to overcome the fact that she is her own worst enemy; in other words, she is both the lead and the antagonist. Perhaps her costar is tired of living with someone so insecure, or her boss wishes she'd assert herself at meetings because he knows she has a lot to contribute, or her personal trainer is tired of seeing her sabotage herself, or her friend is sick of trying to convince her of how talented she is, or she's in a toxic relationship but won't leave because "she loves him."

When you are not living in alignment with your true self, suppressing your dreams, living with frustration, trying to conform to someone else's version of what life should look like, and remaining stuck with your inner film critic and her fears and self-doubts, you can become your own antagonist—to yourself, and in turn, to someone else—meaning, you are now venturing into the realm of antagonism that you *can* control.

Star

To be a star is to design your life according to what works for you and your family. It could mean living in the limelight as a performer, just as much as it could mean keeping it simple. Being a star to you could be completely different from what it means to me. What's in your heart? Do you desire a quiet life where you enjoy your work, your children, your friends, and your hobbies? Do you have a passion for singing, writing, or becoming a total rock star in your professional life? No matter what you truly desire, as a star, you are self-confident, full of self-esteem, and lead from the heart. When you walk into a room, it is with your head held high. If someone even tries to look down on you, cast you aside, or treat you with indifference, you stand up to them. You choose to surround yourself with people who build you up, not knock you down. You partner with people who are proud to be with you and who add to your life, instead of adding more work to your life.

You holds others up, support them, defend them, and encourage them to feel good. You are proud of your achievements and can face life's challenges with confidence. You are humble and willing to learn new things. As the lead character in your life, you take center stage and want others to do the same. You are authentic and real. You love your-self, not in a narcissistic way, but in a healthy, admirable way. You take care of yourself. You don't judge others, but use good judgment when it comes to whom you allow in your close circle. Most important, you don't try to follow the prescribed path. You carve your own.

To be in your star power is to be in healthy relationships and right livelihood, and to value your health and home.

What it all comes down to is loving yourself. You take care of your body, mind, and spirit. You indulge your creative side, because you know it's an important part of who you are. It isn't about the finished product. You get plenty rest and sleep. I recently had the pleasure of listening to Arianna Huffington, founder of the largest on-line news site *The Huffington Post*, speak at the Massachusetts Conference for Women. I was happy to hear that not only is she a big advocate for getting plenty of sleep, but she has two nap rooms at *Huff Post* and planned to create more because the two they have are frequently booked. Since I started working from home, I've taken twenty-minute naps during the day, which is much healthier than what most people do when their energy slumps (and what I used to do when I worked in an office to avoid falling asleep at my desk)—eat sugar. Many cultures around the world honor the body's natural rhythms. I think it's time we did, too, starting with at least eight hours of rest each night. Studies have shown that sleep deprivation is on par with, if not worse than, driving while drunk. It's used as a torture technique. Yet people will brag about how little sleep they need. This is absurd. Sleep! Stars get plenty of beauty rest.

What does being a star mean to you? A client of mine, Lisa, admitted that the idea of being a star made her feel like a fraud. This is extremely common, especially among women. She was exploring the idea of running workshops on alternative healing, but her conventional background in pharmacology had her inner critic screaming, "Who are *you* to do that?" Even though she had a Ph.D., she still thought she didn't have enough credentials. Her inner film critic automatically pressured her into feeling as though being a star meant being on stage and the center of attention, which wasn't her personality at all. When she learned that it was about designing life on her own terms, according to her own values and what she wanted for her life, and that the "fraud" feelings were simply her inner critic's way of getting her to play movie extra in her life story, she was able to move forward.

The Fourth Chakra: Heart

The fourth chakra, or heart chakra, is the chakra between the three lower chakras pertaining to matter and the three above which pertain to spirit. This is the chakra of love and relationships. It is the chakra of balance. Its element is air, its color is green and pink, and its demon is *grief.*

The heart chakra pertains to the heart and circulatory system, lungs, shoulders and arms, ribs/breasts, diaphragm, and thymus gland.

Someone with a balanced, healthy heart chakra loves herself enough to go after what feels right to her instead of what she's been told she's supposed to want for her life. She is compassionate, empathetic, and joyful. She is able to connect with people on a physical, mental, and spiritual level. She is nonjudgmental.

Someone with an imbalanced heart chakra may be critical. She doesn't love or appreciate who she is. Lacking self-esteem, she will tend to do more than she should in relationships in the hopes that whatever self-love she lacks can be filled by somebody else—something that never works. She may become codependent and allow herself to be manipulated into doing things that are damaging to her life in order to hold onto a relationship. The relationship becomes a replacement for the lack of love she has for herself. Too overcome with guilt, she is stuck.

In step three, *Become a Producer*, you could see in each story how money, sex, and creativity (career, work, art) are connected. When these connections are unhealthy, not only can they do damage in the second chakra, but in the heart chakra as well. When you are in an unhealthy relationship where you've either abdicated personal responsibility for your career or your financial decision-making, or even allowed another person to dictate what is a worthwhile creative endeavor, it may be because you are overcome with guilt just thinking about claiming what's rightfully yours—namely sovereignty over your own affairs *where it belongs*. But the prospect of possibly losing a relationship because you chose to love yourself first can create deep, heartfelt grief as well. No wonder people get trapped in bad relationships.

Self-love extends beyond just how you interact with others on an intimate level. It also happens when you choose to create your own work life and decide to leave jobs that are harmful to your health, and when you decide to feed your body with good food, make time for exercise, and love yourself enough to relax and do things for the pure enjoyment of it.

Love is an important part of Dorothy's journey in *The Wizard of Oz*. In her dream she comes across the tin man who says he doesn't have a heart, symbolic perhaps of the idea that Dorothy is brokenhearted over the fact that the two people she trusted most, Auntie Em and Uncle Henry, allowed Gulch to take away her beloved dog, Toto. She has hardened her heart (he is made of tin—a hard exterior shell) and needs to open it up again. She surrounds herself with love and support as she makes her way to the Emerald City—green, the color of the heart chakra. "Home is where the heart is." Interesting that one of the worst things the tin man can do is cry because it makes him rust, thus immobilizing him. Crying is a natural reaction to grief, the demon of the heart chakra.

If our biography is our biology, then maintaining a healthy energetic system requires us to deal with our thoughts and emotions. An imbalance in the heart chakra can be linked to heart and lung problems, breast cancer, and issues in the upper back and shoulders. Loving yourself heals the heart chakra. Unfortunately, there's so much pressure in our society to "be" somebody, "do" something amazing, and "have abundance", meaning tons of money. The result is a whole lot of people running around feeling disconnected from the things that truly make us happy—like true love, friendships, and simple pleasures. While grief is considered the demon of this chakra, I believe it is also suppressed grief which is the true demon, not just grief itself, because grief is our way through heartbreak. One of my clients lost his son to a drug overdose and he cried and cried for a long time. When friends urged him to go on medication, he refused and said, "In order to heal, you have to feel." I think many people grieve without knowing it. We think of grief only in terms of how we feel when a person dies. But we also grieve the loss of things like spare time.

Heartache, loss, pain, and grief are certainly emotions none of us want to experience, but emotion is part of being human. Healing the heart chakra requires feeling grief, so that it may pass through us and transform us. But it requires that we take action *first*. Feelings follow action, so doing what's wise—because you know deep down that it is right for you in the long run—will bring your heart chakra into balance. And sometimes the best action you can take is to choose not to act at all, but to wait, reassess, and then make your move.

Amanda and Iris in *The Holiday* have similar act one challenges. They've both experienced romantic loss. But this is just the situation. The inside story is that both women are not behaving like leading ladies in their love lives. Iris is more like the supporting player, or the best friend, as Arthur Abbott describes it. She is always there for Jasper, even though he is a selfish jerk who strings her along. Amanda is more like an antagonist in her own life. Her heart has become so hardened as a result of her parent's divorce that she cannot cry. She is the tin woman. Each woman suppresses grief in her own way: Iris by kidding herself that she can be Jasper's friend, and Amanda by pushing men away as a way to prevent heartbreak. If she pushes them away first, they cannot hurt her.

I love *The Holiday* because Iris and Amanda are on vacation to grieve. The action they take is to stop acting and go on vacation. They vacate their lives and begin to see things from an entirely different viewpoint. It is through self-love that they are able to attract their true loves. They take center stage as leading ladies to open their hearts to men who are more deserving of their affections.

Amanda and Iris's Transformation

ACT 2

Mind
Amanda and Iris
Become Stars/Leading
Ladies

Courage
Amanda to be vulnerable,
Iris to find gumption to
end it with Jasper

Heart
Love themselves enough
to take a vacation
Fall in love again

ACT 1

ACT 3

Challenge:
Grief over breakups

Resolution:
New relationships with
men who are better
matches

The Unsinkable Molly Brown

After being unemployed for nearly two years, losing her husband of 30 years shortly after she had been laid off, having one child in college, and feeling frightened that she wasn't going to find a job in time to keep from losing her home, Molly finally found work. To say she was relieved would have been an understatement. She settled into the new position without about as much internal ease as a war refugee who'd just stepped off the plane and onto American soil for the first time, not knowing any English, and having no idea what was to come.

Molly poured herself into the new job, determined to know the product she was going to teach new clients how to use, inside and out. She spent hours studying the company's documentation and tutorials, sat in on calls, and stayed in the office long after everyone else had gone home to make sure she got it all right, right down to the letter.

"What time do they shut the lights off? Because I was here at nine o'clock and all of a sudden the lights went out and I had to find my way out of the building in the dark," Molly asked.

I was the Manager of Customer Success, and she was one of my consultants.

"Why were you here so late?" I asked.

Molly explained that she needed to work that late in order to understand everything. She created job aids and checklists, and offered to share them so that I may add them to the new employee certification program I'd built. If she was going to be up and running, this is what she felt she had to do.

I explained to Molly that no one expected her to get it that quickly. New consultants typically spent at least six to eight weeks in training. It was as though Molly needed to beat the average, even though it wasn't necessary.

It turned out that Molly had a few other things going on as well. She needed knee replacement surgery. Standing up, sitting down, and walking—activities most of us do without giving it a thought, were a workout for Molly. She'd wince when she stood up after sitting for an extended period of time, and it was as though she needed to warm up her legs before finding her stride, just to walk across the office to go to the ladies room.

On the outside, she was always put together. Molly's hair was short, blonde, and always in place. Her makeup was done, complete with eye shadow, mascara, and lipstick. She dressed impeccably and wore the most gorgeous jewelry that she picked up for a song at one of those best-kept-secrets kinds of places. While she could be direct, to the point, and abrupt, she also had the markings of a loyal friend—the kind you could act goofy with, who wouldn't judge you, and who would make you laugh for hours. But there was no telling Molly what to do. When I told her to leave no later than six o'clock and to take breaks, she looked at me like I was from another planet— a slacker boss in one way, a dream manager in another. Molly came from a corporate culture that expected late hours, and now she was working for a single mother who'd spent her entire career advocating for work/life balance, and who'd succeeded in a corporate environment putting in a standard, forty-hour work week, sometimes even less.

Molly settled into the new job, but continued with her late hours and vigilant record keeping, lest she leave something out. She was determined to do nothing to compromise what was promising to be her dream job. Helping customers made her happy. Seeing them get excited about their projects and off to a great start fueled her.

I moved into a new role, and a year later, I went part-time to start my *Star in Your Own Life Story* business. Molly, to my surprise, joined my first course. She confided in me that back when I told her she needed to cut back on her hours, she was insulted. I guess I was her antagonist! But after I left, she had to work for a new boss, and this is when the you-know-what hit the fan.

Molly called me, upset over contradictory performance reviews. Her manager gave her a good review, but his boss told Molly that his review didn't count. He told her she wasn't doing her job, but wouldn't elaborate on why, and then said he could hire two people for less than what he was paying her. It turns out that she often kept client praise to herself, and the only thing that made its way to the big boss's desk was a couple of complaints. One of those complaints was concocted by a sales rep and could have easily been remedied had she spoken directly to Molly. He said nothing to uplift Molly, and basically told her there would be no promotional opportunities for her, even if she "perfected" her current role.

This was a huge blow, but it was also a big wake-up call. Molly's antagonist was her boss's boss. What her antagonist was teaching her, although he didn't realize it, was that she was great at playing a supporting role to her clients, but she was a complete extra when it came to singing her own praises. Molly was also proving to be her own antagonist when it came to her overall life. She was completely out of balance with her time, and she was ignoring her health and well-being.

It's easy to understand how it got this way. Molly's primary motivation was fear. She was afraid to go home to an empty house. She was afraid to have knee replacement surgery. She was afraid that she'd lose her job if she didn't do it *perfectly* and *prove* how valuable she was by her willingness to work at all hours of the day and night. She checked and rechecked to make sure she dotted every I and crossed every T. Molly was also still grieving the death of her husband. By failing to strike a balance between her work and personal life, she wound up doing the exact opposite of what she'd intended. Molly needed a strong dose of self-love.

Things started to turn around when she learned about the ruby slippers, and remembered her experience with the *Unsinkable Molly Brown*.

"Stay tight inside of them. They must be very powerful, or she wouldn't want them so badly," said Glinda to Dorothy, waving her wand at her feet. Just as the wicked witch was an outward manifestation of Dorothy's fear, Molly's boss was hers, and Molly could feel her self-confidence waning as a result of her interactions with him.

From then on, Molly made a conscious decision to keep tight inside her own ruby slippers. She started connecting with people on LinkedIn and updated her resume, just in case things didn't work out in her current job. She talked about scheduling a trip with her sister-in-law. She sent all client praise to her manager instead of keeping it to herself. By six o'clock, at the latest, she was out the door. During the day, she would take a walk, sometimes just to her car to sit in silence for a while.

Molly also completed one of the scriptwriting exercises in my on-line course called *Flashback*. When Molly shared her writing, she prefaced it by saying she was tired of talking about work. She wasn't sure why, but when she started writing, something from her teen years appeared on the page. She decided to write about the time she tried out for the lead role in a high school play, *The Unsinkable Molly Brown*. Her friend got the part, a girl who was a couple grades older and who had more acting experience. Molly was clearly disappointed that she didn't get to play Molly, but she described how she made the best of her supporting role, the funny but unnoticeable mistakes she made, and all the fun they had back then. Still, undercutting the positive words Molly used to describe that time in her life was a sense of uneasiness. What interested me was why this play, performed forty years ago, was still so fresh in her memory. As I said in the introduction to this book, there's a reason why we carry certain stories around with us. They contain clues to our present moment. Sometimes these are hints at what may be holding us back, and other stories hold clues about our life purpose. I knew there were some clues in Molly's experience with *The Unsinkable Molly Brown*.

What wasn't clear to Molly at first, but what was revealing itself to me, was how she carried the same feelings about not being the chosen one and of "losing out" to someone with more experience, into her adult work life. Molly was always striving to do more and to *perfect* her role and prove she was "worthy of the part". Funny that she should attract a manager who was waiting for her to do the same thing! It was as though she was continually trying out for the lead part and never getting it. In her mind, she needed to still work on it—to do more to prove herself, because *there would always be the girl with more acting experience*. For her own sake, both personally and professionally, she needed to trust more, to let go, become more efficient, and share client praise with her manager instead of filing it away on her computer under the guise of humility (another manifestation of the need to be perfect, i.e., good people don't brag).

Molly began to see how she *was* the Unsinkable Molly Brown. Molly persevered through life's toughest challenges—layoff, death of a loved one, illness, and being on the brink of financial ruin. Nothing could keep her down. Whatever cards life dealt, Molly always came back with a winning hand. When she told her personal story, she was able to gain a fresh perspective, realize the job wasn't the end-all, be-all, and that she was going to be okay. She also spoke to her doctor and scheduled an appointment for her first knee replacement surgery.

"I didn't realize it, but I guess I was scared to have the procedure. I don't know what it was, but it was like a light turned on, and I was no longer afraid. You never know when you're going to go. You have to live each day to the fullest!" she said.

Molly became her own life story's heroine. She stopped listening to her inner film critic, who loved to tell her she was never working hard enough. She listened to her inner director instead, who told her she was a great employee who deserved to enjoy her life. It turns out that Molly's antagonist was really just mirroring her own internal beliefs around the fallacy that her work would never be as good as someone else's. She overcame her fear of losing her job and found the courage to not only schedule the surgery she needed, but to take time off. She opened her heart again, not in a romantic sense, but to herself. She loved herself enough to take care of her own health and well-being.

Did everyone react positively to her newfound spirit? Not initially, but Molly knows that's outside her control. What's within her control is how she chooses to respond to her manager and what life script she'll follow, and it is with a smile on her face and her head held high.

Playing the inspiring lead character in her own life story wasn't something Molly had to try out for; it was there for her all along. All she had to do was step into her power and take center stage, because when it comes to your own life, you can't help but play the lead role, it's just that you sometimes forget and act more like an extra, best friend, or antagonist.

Molly donned her ruby slippers, found with her not-so-cowardly lion, and faced those fears head-on. She connected with fear's antidote, *courage,* overcame false beliefs that told her she wasn't enough, and gave herself the love and attention she deserved. In other words, she connected with her courage, heart, and mind, just like a great movie heroine, and with amazing results.

Summary

There are times in life when you play the role of an extra, supporting player, and antagonist. The key is to be mindful of when you are acting out these parts not because it is appropriate or outside of your control (i.e., when you are the source of someone's envy), but because you're afraid to shine as the star in your life story.

Review the first four steps. Examine the kind of script you're writing for your life, any shadow aspects of your archetypes that you need to release, and imbalances in your second chakra, where you may not be paying attention to your creative side or you're ignoring your finances or career. Notice when you're listening to your inner film critic, who prefers that you stay stuck where you are and take a backseat, rather than play full-out. Continue to tune into the voice of your inner film director, because she is your wise guide. Not only will she always encourage you to be the star, but she will also point you in the direction you need to go and to what you need to do to shine the brightest.

Part of bringing your heart chakra into a healthy state of balance is to find your voice—just as Dorothy stands up to the Wicked Witch of the West—a metaphor for finding her voice and facing her fears. In the next chapter, *Learn Your Lines, Lead with Assertiveness*, you'll learn how.

Notes

Notes

STEP SIX

Learn Your Lines

Lead with Assertiveness

The King's Speech

Lionel sits down on the chair of Edward the Confessor.

> BERTIE
> What are you doing? Get up!
> You can't sit there.
> *Overlapping-*

> LIONEL
> Why not? It's a chair.

> BERTIE
> No it's not, that's Saint Edward's chair—

> LIONEL
> People have carved their initials into it!

> BERTIE
> That chair is the seat upon which
> every king and queen—

> LIONEL
> It's held in place by a large rock!

> BERTIE
> That is the stone of scone, you
> are trivializing everything—

> LIONEL
> I don't care. I don't care how many
> royal arses have sat in this chair.
> *Overlapping-*

                    BERTIE
               Listen to me…!

                    LIONEL
          Listen to you! By what right?

                    BERTIE
    Divine right, if you must! I'm your king!

                    LIONEL
      Nooo, you're not. Told me so yourself.
      Said you didn't want it. So why should
         I waste my time listening to you?

                    BERTIE
        Because I have a right to be heard!

                    LIONEL
               Heard as what?

                    BERTIE
          As a man! I HAVE A VOICE!

                    LIONEL
                   (quietly)
    Yes, you do. You have such perseverance,
    Bertie, you're the bravest man I know.
      And you'll make a bloody good king.

The King's Speech

On the opening scene of *The King's Speech*, Prince Albert struggles to speak because of his debilitating stammer. His wife goes to see Lionel Logue, a speech coach, to see if he can help her husband. Prince Albert's challenge is to overcome his speech impediment in order to address the people of England live and over the radio.

His brother is an irresponsible playboy unfit to be king, even though he is next in line to the throne. Their father is ill. Bertie knows that the inevitable outcome is that he'll have to assume the role, but he's fearful and he doubts his competence. The shadow side of the prince archetype is the reluctant leader who questions his ability to lead. Albert is living in the shadow of his inner prince—in this case, he is a literal prince. At first, he thinks the exercises Lionel makes him go through are ridiculous and tells Lionel he isn't coming back.

Bertie listens to Lionel's recording of his voice, and much to his amazement, he doesn't hear any stammer, so he returns for coaching. Bertie confides to Lionel that he was abused by a nanny when he was a little boy around the time his stammer started. Since then, he's had a hard time asserting himself—having a voice. But he still resists Lionel's help, sticking only with physical exercises. He opens himself to receiving help, but only on a surface level. Anything "royal" is off limits. Bertie is a bit of a snob and won't allow himself to become Lionel's friend. He rejects Lionel when he crosses a line and implies that Bertie would make a good king when it's getting clearer that his brother is unfit.

In the final act, Bertie is about to be crowned the king, when his advisors inform him that Lionel isn't a doctor. Bertie tries to reject his help because he lacks this credential, until he finds Lionel sitting on a royal chair, as you read in the opening script in this chapter. (The movie clip is included in your Star Pack.)

This becomes a turning point in the movie, where we can see that he's about to overcome his past conditioning and learn to assert himself. He fully opens to receiving the help of Lionel and stands up to the archbishop when he tries to dismiss him.

In the end, the king successfully delivers a radio address to Britain with Lionel coaching him throughout. He continued to inspire his country during WWII, and he and Lionel remain friends throughout their lives.

Learn Your Lines
Lead with Assertiveness

*T*he sixth step to starring in your own life story, *Learn your Lines, Lead with Assertiveness*, is about having a voice in every area of your life. The chakra associated with this step is the fifth or throat chakra.

When you decide to play the lead character of your life story, you must first become an actor. As an actor, you play another role and respond the way your character would respond as a confident, victorious star, instead of a supporting player, extra, or victim. You're going to learn what it means to truly embody the character who is able to take the lead in her life and speak with assertiveness. You must respond as someone who is in full command of herself, as someone who will not put up with injustice, and as someone who asserts herself and tells the truth, no matter what. It won't feel natural if you're not used to it—you need to practice until you get the hang of it. Keep in mind that this isn't about becoming a different person but about changing your strategy.

Everything you learned to do in your life felt unnatural at first. Think about the first time you got on a bicycle without training wheels, played piano, or got behind the wheel of a car. New things feel awkward at first, until they become habit. Learning to become a star communicator is no different. This is when you gain some acting experience. You've heard the expression, "Fake it till you make it." This step is all about becoming a better listener and learning your lines—your assertive lines. It's about temporarily becoming an actor, until your new way of being forms a better you.

I once took an acting class, and I remember thinking about how hard it must be for actors to remember their lines. I have always been in awe of lead characters who could memorize the lines in a two-hour play. A big part of acting is listening. The expression, "God gave you two ears and one mouth for a reason" reminds us that if we spend twice as much time listening as we do speaking, we'll be better off. Actors don't just memorize their lines; they listen intently to the lines delivered by their costars for cues to what comes next. Anyone in sales will tell you that their success comes from listening to the prospect or client, not just talking about your product or service. By hearing what someone is saying, a stellar salesperson becomes a consultant and true helper. The sale happens naturally.

The same can be said for relationships—whether it's with a significant other, a child, a person you just met, or the people you work with, everyone loves to be heard. Before you deliver your lines, it's a good idea to practice the art of becoming a good listener. Here are some things good listeners do.

Lean in

When you are speaking to someone, show them that you are interested in them and what they have to say through your body language.

Restate

Paraphrase what they are telling you with statements like, "So what I hear you saying is..."

Ask questions

Ask them to elaborate, tell you more, or to clarify something. When it is your turn to speak, be assertive. The following describes the difference between a passive, passive-aggressive, aggressive, and an assertive communicator.

Passive Communicator

A person who is passive says nothing rather than getting into an argument or situation where she may have to persuade the other person. She's submissive to the point of doing things she does not want to do because of an inability to say *no*. Because of this submissive behavior, she often ends up frustrated. Over time this can result in problems pertaining to the throat chakra, which you'll read about in a little while. Prince Albert was passive to the point of stuttering. Perhaps you have a bit of the shadow prince in you. This is natural if you've just taken on a managerial role, but like the king, you need to find your voice in order to lead.

Passive-Aggressive Communicator

A passive-aggressive communicator is indirect, manipulative, sneaky, and devious. Rather than being submissive or outright aggressive, the person who is passive-aggressive will do things such as slam doors, make sarcastic comments without giving the receiver a chance to respond, interrupt, leave the room to avoid the other person's reaction, or shout things while passing by. She doesn't generally tell the other person what she wants to say. She may make sarcastic and negative comments, give off an attitude of smugness, and use negative body language such as eye-rolling, avoiding eye contact with the other person, or casting a "knowing" glance at someone else. She may also do things behind the person's back and then lie about it. Passive-aggression is an insidious form of behavior. You wouldn't want someone in your life who acts like this, so it's definitely something to avoid in your own communication patterns as well. If you find yourself doing passive-aggressive things, think about what is causing you to act that way. What are you afraid of? Are you jealous, angry, or bitter? What are you afraid to say?

Aggressive

The aggressive communicator acts as though the only way to get what she wants is to shout, point fingers, or otherwise intimidate the other person. An aggressive person approaches situations as if they were contests: only one person can win, and she must be the winner. The aggressive person is not interested in a "win-win" situation. She is only interested in her own point of view. Acts of aggression can be physical or verbal. Making threatening gestures or attempting to control another person physically (either through outright harm or by restricting their movements) are examples.

Aggression is an indication of a person's need to be right at all costs. Any notion that someone else may have a point feels like a threat, so the aggressive person reacts by yelling, being sarcastic, making belittling remarks, shaming, controlling, interrupting, or nonstop talking so that no one can get a word in edgewise. Aggression is something a person may lead up to. Joe started to purposely bump into my elbow when he walked by because he didn't like it when I stood at the stove with my hand on my hip. I wasn't even aware that I did it. He later graduated to poking me hard in the upper arm when I went to open the refrigerator door.

Whether the aggression is verbal or physical, you don't want to be around an aggressive person, so don't be that person.

"During Amy's course, we discussed assertive messages, which particularly resonated with me. I have a tendency to be direct and aim for the throat. I realized through doing the assertiveness assessment that I can be very aggressive when it comes to how I speak to my kids and my boyfriend. I never meant to come across as mean, but that night I learned to express how I feel in a much more effective way.

"I feel this way" brought me much better results than saying things like, "You make me feel this" or "You are doing that". It truly helped me professionally, and more importantly, with my children and boyfriend. As a result of my newfound assertiveness, we grew closer. It was an eye opener for me and I so appreciated the input."

—Doreen

Assertive

When someone is assertive, she is confident, honest, and straightforward. She's respectful. The terms "aggressive" and "assertive" are often used interchangeably as if they mean the same thing, but as you know, they are not. Unlike the aggressive communicator, the assertive person is able to get her point across without resorting to abusive, intimidating behavior.

To become more assertive, make sure you are employing all the steps you've learned to this point. Listen to your inner director, not to the voice of your inner film critic, who may instill fear in you and tell you that in order to keep the peace, you have to stay silent, or to get your way, you have to scream and shout. Have faith that being assertive is in your highest and best good, not something to be feared. Keep in mind that you must act if you are going to bring about the changes you desire, and the more you do it, the more confident you'll become. Speaking assertively is an act of appreciation. Not only are you respecting the person you're talking to, but you're creating a better environment for communication, which will benefit you as well. The more you do it, the better you get at it.

To be an excellent communicator, strive to have strong body language: a commanding presence that reflects confidence, high self-esteem, and charisma. Stand up straight, shoulders back; take a deep breath and tune in to your wise, intuitive self. Keep in mind that just because you become more assertive does not mean that the people in your life will automatically do what you want or react the way you'd like them to. The goal is to stop suppressing your feelings and to feel good about yourself. When you do, you'll realize that acting was what you had been doing all along. Speaking your truth is *who you are*. You're no longer faking it.

Lionel may have brought Albert through a series of physical exercises to help him overcome his stammer, but it was Bertie's increased confidence and ability to stand up for himself—to assert himself—that made the biggest difference. "I have a voice."

The Fifth Chakra: Throat

The fifth chakra, or throat chakra, is the chakra of communication and sound—vibration. It's related to the throat, thyroid, trachea, neck vertebrae, mouth, teeth and gums. Those with excessive amounts of fifth chakra energy cannot stop talking and may speak aggressively. Those who are deficient may suffer from a fear of speaking up—they are passive. The color of the fifth chakra is blue. Its element is sound. Its demon is lies.

Assertiveness results in a healthy fifth chakra. Think of a variety of situations where you are challenged in this way. For example, if you met someone who you were romantically interested in, would you have the courage to walk up to them and suggest you meet for a cup of coffee sometime, or would you be too afraid? In a meeting at work, would you sit silently and wait for someone to call on you, or would you speak up, and even disagree with someone, if you felt the situation called for it? Are you afraid to tell your partner the truth? Do you hold back when something is bothering you because you're afraid they will leave you, or they won't be able to survive without you? Do you have trouble telling other people about the creative projects you're passionate about? On the other hand, are there situations where you don't think before you speak and wind up yelling or ridiculing the other person?

Saying what's on your mind and sensing another's vibes are related to this energy center. Your voice is how you express your vibration. If you are afraid to speak up, or your preferred mode of communication is to shout, you are closing down this energy center. If you lie, you become out of alignment in your body. And I don't just mean lying to someone else, but lying to yourself as well. Are you lying to yourself about the reality of your job and how it makes you feel? How about your relationships? Are you kidding yourself that a weight problem doesn't have a negative impact on your health or your home environment is okay when it isn't? Lying is not only bad for relationships, but bad for your health. Mantras and affirmations may work on the mind, but they also work on this energy center, because they are spoken aloud. It is the vibration and energy of the fifth chakra that you connect with.

All of the writing exercises in this program help to bring your chakras into alignment, but the act of writing in particular can help to open up the throat chakra, because it involves telling your story. Journal writing, talking to a coach, therapist, or counselor, and ultimately telling others your core story—the story of you, helps to open up this energy center. Keeping stories bottled up inside or neglecting to express your true feelings can create health problems in this area of your body. Telling your story can unblock this energy center, resulting in a healthy throat chakra.

Chanting and singing are also healthy ways to balance your throat chakra. The sound of "Om" in yoga class has a purpose. You can read the definition we provide students at the Open Doors studio where I teach in the box on this page. When Jack was a baby, I could often hear him making random noises when he awoke from his nap. I'd go in his room and he'd be lying on his back in the crib holding onto his feet; "happy baby pose" as we refer to it in yoga. He made all sorts sounds, testing out his voice. He'd grin from ear to ear when he saw me. When he started walking, he'd come right up to you and carry on a conversation in gibberish. I'm certain he knew what he was saying, but we had no clue. I started singing to Jack and Christopher when they were babies and couldn't leave their bedroom until I sang every nursery rhyme I knew. This went on for about ten years. I wasn't thinking about it much when I started. All I knew is that it reduced my anxiety when they cried, and when I did it they'd calm down. I'd sing them to sleep. I'd sing to them at the park. According to neuropsychologist Sally Blythe from the lullaby project in the neonatal ward of the Royal London Hospital, singing prepares a child's voice, brain, and ear for language.

Taking center stage and starring in your own life story means that you don't suppress your voice, keep quiet when you have something to say, or compromise your values, nor does it mean you are offensive, nosy, gossipy, or speak your mind without taking other people's feelings into account. To be assertive means you know how to say something without harming the esteem of another, you understand boundaries, and you respect people's feelings and beliefs, including your own.

In act 1 of *The King's Speech*, we learn that Prince Albert, the movie's protagonist, has a speech impediment (his challenge and antagonist) because of childhood abuse, bullying, and dismissive attitudes from his brother and other people in his life. He connects with his courage by humbling himself enough to accept the help of his speech coach, and then he stands up to Lionel and then for himself when he refuses to allow the archbishop to fire Lionel. Prince Albert (who became King George) had to find his voice in order to take center stage in his role as a king during a time of war.

No matter what your role is, no matter how seemingly insignificant it may seem in comparison to a king, assert yourself. It will benefit not only you, but those around you as well.

"OM can have a secular or non-secular meaning. In secular terms, it is a way to calm and prepare the mind before and after class. It reminds us that we are all here, together, and can be a very unifying experience. In non-secular terms, the four individual sounds of OM (Ah, Oh, MMM, and silence) represent the four states of consciousness and use a human voice to reproduce a sound which is continuously being produced by the universe. OM is a sound that represents your understanding of a higher power and that higher power's connection to you." Open Doors, MA

King George's Transformation

ACT 2

Mind
Believes he has
a voice and is
qualified to be king

Courage
Confronts painful child-
hood memories

Heart
Befriends a commoner.
Appreciates himself

ACT 1

ACT 3

Challenge:
Stammer

Resolution:
Delivers inspirational
speeches during WWII

Summary

Learning your lines is about becoming an actor—doing the uncomfortable thing of pretending to be assertive until speaking your mind becomes natural. Acting, it turns out, is what you do when you *don't* speak the truth. Assertiveness in all areas of your life results in a healthy throat chakra. If you ever choke on your words, experience tightness in your chest because you're not saying what's on your mind, pretend to be someone you're not, or feel bad because of a lie, then take a look at the relationship and ask yourself what's preventing you from being assertive.

If you're ready to go a step further, join the *Star in Your Own Life Story* course. We do a guided visualization, a yoga pose that opens up the throat chakra, and explore a series of questions that will help you to identify areas where you want to become more assertive. You will have access to a character assertiveness assessment where you can assess how well you assert yourself in six different areas of your life, thereby identifying relationships where you may have lost your voice and would benefit from getting it back. You'll also have access to a tip sheet, outlining ten specific ways you can become more assertive, and my interview with Enneagram expert, Steven Eric Connors, along with a guide to the Enneagram. This thousands-of-years-old tool will help you to identify your dominant personality type. It also will explain why people communicate the way they do, and you will gain insight into yourself as well as the people you interact with. I have taken many assessments over the years including Myers Briggs, the DISC, and numerous others, and the Enneagram is by far my favorite. I'm a type Seven, Enthusiast. What's your type? You can find out more about this program by going to www. StarInYourOwnLifeStory.com/course

Assertiveness would come easily if you didn't have to deal with any difficult people, right? In the next chapter, you're going to Find Your Supporting Players and Lead with a Team. You'll begin to call into your life people you can be yourself with, who are easy to talk to, and who will benefit your life on every level.

Meet Lois, my Antagonist

Whether your story's antagonist is a passive-aggressive co-worker, a parent specializing in guilt trips, a partner giving you a hard time, or a rebellious child, we all have someone playing this role. They're the ones who keep us up at night, drive us crazy, and bring out our absolute worst. Ever wonder why people act like this? Have they nothing better to do?

I've known quite a few antagonists, but let me tell you about a woman who used to work in human resources at one of my previous places of employment. (I'd name names, but you know how it is.)

Lois walked up to me when I was eight months pregnant. I was practically bursting at the seams, I was so large, not to mention uncomfortable and a bit sensitive. She placed a photograph on my desk that had been taken a few years before.

"Look how skinny you were," she said.

Lois let out an evil chuckle as I glanced down at the former me, the one who taught five step classes a week and fit into a size six; a size I hadn't seen in months and never saw again.

I pretended not to care. I think I may have even thanked her for the picture. Lois derived great pleasure from my rotundness. God only knows what nasty joke she would have played on me, had she known about my chafed inner thighs.

I could have given it right back to her. I could have pointed out the fact that she was the same size I was even though she wasn't pregnant, or asked her if she planned to get hair transplants for her bald spot, but I couldn't bring myself to be that mean. I knew deep down it wasn't about me. She was trying to feel better about herself by making me feel worse.

Lois and I had a history. No matter how nice I was to her, she continually made snide remarks or gave me a hard time. I was just trying to do my job and get along, but Lois wouldn't have any of it. I was always caught off-guard by her nastiness.

When I returned to work after having the baby, I decided I was done taking Lois's crap. Maybe it was motherhood. All I know is I couldn't take another minute of her pettiness. My play-nice strategy clearly didn't work, but I wasn't about to stoop to her level. I needed a better way, and it didn't take long before I was presented with an opportunity to make things right.

My boss assigned me a project that required Lois's team to attach a benefits announcement to 1000 employee paychecks.

"I don't think so. The girls and I (that's how she described the three women on her team) don't like having to do that," she said, and then she turned to walk away.

There was no way I was going to fall into her trap again. Lois expected me to do what I had always done, which would have been to go back to the boss and tell him what she said, and then go back to her to tell her he said she had to. It was a childish game, and I refused to play.

"We all have to do things we don't like to do," I said.

Lois stopped and turned around to face me. I wasn't about to back down. I crossed my arms and stood my ground.

"I don't like everything I have to do either, but I still have to do them," I added.

"I suppose that's true," she said.

"I'll be by later on to drop off the documents," I said.

Lois looked stunned. I said nothing. She walked away, and that was the last time I had problems with her. From then on, she was practically respectful and even asked about my son once in a while. Maybe it was my weight gain, but I like to think it was my new found assertiveness that caused her to change her tune. I had confused passivity with niceness. Learning to stick up for myself was a valuable lesson I may not have learned had it not been for Lois, even though she wasn't doing it for my benefit.

Our antagonists make asserting ourselves a challenge. They may bring out the worst in us, but they also bring out our very best if we let them.

Notes

STEP SEVEN

Find Your Supporting Players

Lead With a Team

Groundhog Day

HAWLEY looks across the studio and sees RITA
HANSON enter, a very attractive segment producer
in her late twenties.

> HAWLEY
> *(to Phil)*
> I'll give you Rita. *(calls her over)*
> Rita, could you come here for a second?
> I got a little job for you.

Rita is relatively new to the station, but compe-
tent, personable, humorous, self-assured,and very
pretty—in short, a genuine princess, though Phil
is too self-absorbed at this point to realize it.

> PHIL
> *(teasing)*
> You can't send Rita out on a story like this.
> She's just a cub, a pup, still wet behind
> the ears. Look at her. Her ears are sopping
> wet. This needs a Woodward or a Bernstein.
> It's a big story. People need to know.

> RITA
> (intrigued)
> What's the story?

> HAWLEY
> The Punxsutawney Groundhog Festival.

> RITA
> Gil, if it's all right with you I'd rather
> follow-up on the nurses' strike.

                         HAWLEY
You can do the nurses when you get back. Just
take the squeaky wheel here up to Punxsutawney
     and get him back in one piece. Okay?

                          RITA
                     Yeah, okay.
       Hawley exits, leaving Phil and Rita alone
        in the studio. She knows Phil mainly by
      his reputation, and it isn't good. Still,
        she finds him appealing in an odd way.

                          PHIL
                     (pleasantly)
You know, this could be extremely interesting.

                          RITA
       I've never done a weather story
        before. What's Punxsutawney like?

                          PHIL
Oh, it's an enchanted place. A magical world.
It's the Constantinople of the whole Western
Appalachian-Susquehanna drainage system.

                          RITA
                Do you always joke?

                          PHIL
About 70 to 80 percent of the time. Inside I'm
    actually a very shy and sensitive person.

                         RITA
            A lot of people around here think
                 you're not very sincere.

                         PHIL
            Tell me the names of these people.

                         RITA
            I'll line up a crew and transportation.
            If you don't feel like driving, we can
            all go up in the van together.

                         PHIL
            I think I'll take my own car. I' m
            not that fond of my fellow man.

                         RITA

                      (exiting)

               Nice attitude.

                         PHIL
                    Nice face.

    (calls after her)

            Why don't you ride up with me?

                         RITA
                    No, thanks.

STEPHANIE DECASTRO, an attractive, dark-eyed,
dark-haired correspondent, glares at Phil from
across the studio.

Groundhog Day

Grab a box of Jujubes if your teeth can take it, or those round chocolates with the little white sprinkles on them that I don't know how to pronounce—nonparallels, nonparayls, nonpareils, because this is one of my extended reviews.

The 1993 movie *Groundhog Day* has become a classic. Forget the fact that it's a quasi-holiday. This movie created a new term. To say that you feel like you're stuck in Groundhog Day has become synonymous with that feeling we all experience from time to time of being bored, stuck in a rut, or stagnant in our lives, as if we are repeating the same day over and over again. It's one of my favorite comedies.

In the movie's first act, we meet Phil Connors (Bill Murray), a weatherman. We know his initial challenge is career stagnation when he mentions on his broadcast that he's headed to Punxsutawney, Pennsylvania, to see if the groundhog sees his shadow. It just so happens that the groundhog is also named Phil.

The anchorwoman asks, "This is your third year in row, isn't it, Phil?" as if to say, *You still haven't been promoted or picked up by another network yet, have you, loser?*

He responds with equal sarcasm, "Four years, actually."

As objective observers, we know that his lack of upward mobility probably has something to do with his arrogance and sarcasm. At one point, he refers to himself as "the talent" to Rita (Andie MacDowell), his producer. Later, when a police officer tells him the road's been shut down due to the blizzard, he calls himself "a celebrity in an emergency," as if his celebrity status should somehow afford him special treatment that would surpass even the weather. He is rude, self-centered, egotistical, and reviled by his co-workers, which is what makes the movie so hilarious. What may be awful to deal with in real life often makes for great comedy in film.

It turns out that the groundhog does see his shadow, which means six more weeks of winter. Phil Connors does his report. He and his crew plan to return home, but a snowstorm forces them to stay another night.

Phil is now faced with a challenge, which becomes the focus of the film. He wakes up the next morning at six to the same song that was playing on the radio the morning before: "I've Got You Babe," by Sonny and Cher. At first he thinks the DJs accidentally played the same tape, but he soon discovers he is repeating the same day.

If you were to look at this as a metaphor, Phil Connors—like Punxsutawney Phil, the groundhog—is about to meet his shadow, or his dark self. And he's stuck in the winter of his life, beginning at six every same-old day—six being symbolic of six weeks of winter. Phil Connors is about to have a dark-night-of-the-soul experience.

Phil's desire at the beginning of the film is career advancement, but he can't seem to move up. So we know he's stuck in a job rut. But a new dilemma emerges. He's stuck in a time trap, his version of Oz. His goal is to figure out how to wake up to a new day. As moviegoers, our delight is in seeing what his character is going to do to solve his problem.

At first, as we move into the second act of the film, Phil Connors's personality doesn't change. He's still a sarcastic jerk, which in real life is awful to deal with, but in a movie is funny to watch. His co-workers may be miserable, but for us, it's actually quite fun to see a guy act like that.

His initial reaction to his problem of reliving Groundhog Day is to become reckless. At one point he says to two men sitting next to him at a bar, "What if you were living the same day over and over, and nothing you did mattered?"

One of them says, "Yep, that pretty much sums it up!"

Then he takes off in a car with them, drives down some train tracks, and gets arrested, only to wake up to the same day repeating itself, symbolic of the fact that there is no easy way out of his problem. Just as Dorothy's house landed on the Wicked Witch of the East, leaving her to face the Wicked Witch of the West, Phil has to figure out a way to deal with the time trap.

That's how many of us feel when we are challenged by something in our own lives that never seems to change—the relationship stays the same or we can't find one that makes us happy, our job stinks, we never advance, we want to start a business, dream of writing a book—whatever, we can't seem to do it.

Every day, Phil bumps into Ned Ryerson, a too-friendly, overenthusiastic insurance salesman—in other words, Phil's antithesis. In the first act, Phil treats him with indifference. He's rude, unaffected by this man who recognizes him from high school. Every time Phil walks away, he steps into the same, slush-filled pothole. And every time, Ned laughs and says, "Watch out for that first step, it's a doozy!"

Phil keeps repeating the same day, acting the same way, and stepping in the same potholes. In other words, he's stuck in his own insanity of repeating the same thing over and over again and expecting a different result. He's living out Einstein's famous quote.

Where Phil is really stuck isn't in his repetitive day, but in his attitude. It's Phil's off-putting personality that makes the movie funny. We can tell that he'll need to change in order to move forward. The time trap is really a metaphor for his career stagnation, and as we soon learn, lack of progress in his evolution of as a man.

Phil gets desperate over the fact that he's stuck, so he tries to kill himself by dropping a toaster in the bathtub, driving a truck off a ravine, and jumping off a cliff, among other things. It's his escape fantasy to the extreme. For you it may manifest itself as a fantasy that you will throw it all in—quit, sell your possessions, and drive across the country. I had a friend who actually wished she'd be laid off, because she wanted to start her own business and fantasized that unemployment would provide her with the capital and freedom to get started. But in reality, she knew that wasn't the best solution. Like most of us, she'd have to start something small on the side until she could escape from her old career.

Phil thinks his lack of advancement stems from something outside of him, like the stupidity or blindness of the networks, and then blames his circumstances on the time trap. Things start to turn around when he begins to see that waking up to the same day may actually have its benefits. He stands up to time by using it to his advantage.

In a sense, he realizes he has godlike powers, but true to form, he uses them selfishly. He robs a Brinks truck, uses his charm and celebrity to score with women, and tries to manipulate Rita by finding out personal information about her and presenting himself as someone he isn't, in order to win her affections.

I'm sure you can think of people you've met who were disingenuous and had a hidden agenda. Phil is only able to connect with people on a second-chakra level, through sex and his questionable allure as a television personality. He also punches Ned in the face every time he sees him. He feels liberated from having to follow any established rules of society, including not hitting somebody just because they annoy you.

Phil is manipulating people and behaving inauthentically, which is just a metaphor for how we all feel when we're changing in a way that isn't in alignment with our true selves. We may be listening to what other people think we should be doing instead of what we really want, for example.

Phil starts avoiding the slush-filled pothole. That first step really is a doozy, but once you've taken it, you're on your way. Just as you may need to start walking around a long-held belief that making money by using your talent is wrong, or it's too late for you to find the relationship you are looking for, or you're over forty so getting in shape again is a lost cause, Phil starts seeing things differently. He challenges the belief that his destiny is outside his control. He starts

> *"If, when you focus upon what you want, you would feel good; and if, when you feel good, you would be in the positive mode of attraction, then would not your most important work be to look for the positive aspects of all things, to look for the parts of all things that are uplifting to you—and to get your attention off any potholes in the streets?"*
>
> *—Esther and Jerry Hicks*

taking a different approach. He chooses a new path. Even though the day itself is the same, he doesn't have to repeat it.

Phil doesn't change his personality, but he alters his strategy. Where at first he saw his situation as outside of his control, now he's seeing how he can take advantage of it.

If you feel like you are repeating the same day over and over again, you may go through life without noticing things—or even people. But by repeating his same day over and over again, Phil's awareness becomes heightened, and as his awareness grows, Phil transforms.

Phil doesn't seem to have an inner film critic because he is like a bull in a china shop. He's completely self-absorbed. But people with big egos are usually covering up some insecurity. It's obvious that he has been falling in love with Rita. But in an endearing scene in which Rita falls asleep beside him, he reveals the fact that he doesn't believe that someone like him could ever have such a wonderful woman.

Now we've gotten to the core of Phil's problems. He doesn't think he's worthy of love. This is Phil's inside story—the story he's been telling himself all along. You start to see that his behavior is simply a cover up for his insecurities.

If he wants to get unstuck, then he'll have to write a new life script.

Many of us desire to move from act 1 of our story straight to act 3 without having to do any internal work. When it doesn't happen, we do nothing and stay stuck, wishing and hoping that something will save us from our plight. It's a glass-slipper solution that we all know doesn't work in real life. Sex, thievery, and punching someone in the face may provide some temporary satisfaction, but they are just Band-Aids on Phil's wounded soul.

Phil Connors finds some success in his approach because in some ways he's beginning to get what he wants, but he realizes it's still empty.

What he really wants is the love and affection of Rita. He has managed to develop shallow relationships with the people around him, but he's realizing that what he truly desires is depth and connection.

But his strategies aren't working with Rita. At this point in the film, he's mustered the courage to face his fears of being stuck in Groundhog Day. He's changed his mind about it and altered his strategy for dealing with the situation, but he still hasn't quite arrived at the thing that will make him happy. This brings us to a particular belief of our inner film critic that often keeps us stuck in our act 1 challenge, and why I decided to choose this film for step seven: the belief that you should be able to find a solution to your challenge by yourself.

At the beginning of the story, Phil doesn't connect with people and shows no interest in having friends. He is disconnected from his humanity and need for love. He's built a wall around his heart and lived a hermit's life.

For you, this can show up as a feeling of isolation, a sense that nobody else can help. You should somehow be able to figure it all out on your own and get yourself out of this mess. People can spend years trying to figure it out this way with little or no results. Albert Einstein also said that you can't solve a problem with the same consciousness that created it. So we have two dynamics here—one that says we can't keep repeating the same thing over and over again and another that tells us that we need to change our consciousness.

Essentially, Phil Connors cannot stop the insanity of repeating Groundhog Day until he alters his beliefs about what he truly deserves and opens his heart to love. He must embrace his vulnerability, find the courage to confront his fear of rejection, and learn to love himself in order to understand that he is lovable.

Phil's antagonist, the time trap, arrived just in time to teach him the value of human connection.

When Phil realizes that changing his strategy helps but still isn't winning the heart of Rita, he truly begins to get a life. He turns his energy outward and begins to see how knowing exactly what will happen every day can be used not to help him, but to help others.

He tries to save a homeless man from dying. He catches a boy falling from a tree. He prevents a man from choking. He also becomes more interesting. He learns to speak French and play the piano, and instead of punching the overly-friendly insurance guy, Ned, he buys every kind of insurance Ned is selling. Phil starts to connect with people on an emotional level and becomes more human. By helping them, he helps himself. He may be trapped reliving Groundhog Day, but he learns how to make each day unique. When he stops trying to manipulate people; when he becomes a more interesting person; when he starts helping people; when he gets in touch with his life purpose and with what's in his heart—the desire to have real friends and a deep, connected, loving relationship—he wins the affections of Rita. Instead of waking up alone to "I've Got You Babe," he actually "gets his babe." He wakes up to a new day with Rita by his side. The song itself is a metaphor for what he's lacking at the beginning of the film and what he finds at the end. It turns out his initial challenge, career stagnation, was a red herring.

Find Your Supporting Players
Lead with a Team

O n *Groundhog Day*, Phil Connors connects with his courage, heart, and mind to transform his life. He manages to succeed in large part because he learns how to relate to his "fellow man." It is by forming healthy relationships that he is able to achieve his true heart's desire.

In this step, you are going to identify your costars—your supporting players who will help you to achieve your life's vision, cheer you on, and encourage you to accept nothing less than the best. Not only will you have an opportunity to look at your outer team, but you'll examine your inner team as well—the archetypes who work alongside your inner film director to keep your thoughts positive and your life headed in the right direction.

In *Be the Star*, you learned what it means to take center stage and star in your own life story, rather than staying dissatisfied with your role as an extra or forever playing best supporting actress in someone else's life. In *Learn Your Lines*, you identified areas where you may need to become more assertive, and you've started practicing a way of communicating that will help you to live a more authentic, empowered life. This step is about gathering support, because support is one of the keys to living a happy life, launching a successful business, taking your career to the next level, and feeling nurtured and cared for in a relationship.

If there's anything more difficult than feeling stuck in your life— whether it's a relationship that isn't working, a job that makes you miserable, in a body that's out of shape, in a home environment that lacks the peace and tranquility you desire, or in a state of inaction when it comes to your creative life, it's feeling as if you're alone. Even when things are going well, we all need the strength and support of good people. In this chapter, you will be introduced to five new archetypes—the hermit, martyr, liberator, lover, and god/goddess—and see how these archetypal companions can help you get unstuck.

Archetypes

The shadow aspects of the first two archetypes I chose for this step mirror Phil Connor's attitude (as shown in the script at the beginning of this chapter): "I'm not that fond of my fellow man." If you can relate to the martyr and hermit, this may be a place where you need to work on your relationship-building skills. That is not to say that if you tend to be a private person and prefer a small network of close friends you suddenly have to become the life of the party with three thousand friends on Facebook, unless of course you're running an on-line business, in which case, the more the merrier (www.StarInYourOwnLifeStory.com/facebookfans).

A positive attitude, warm heart, and open mindset will transform your life, whereas a negative outlook, hardened heart, and closed mind will block your progress and keep you stuck in act 1. The light aspects of the three archetypes which come next, the lover, god/goddess, and liberator will help you open your mind and heart to the joy of connecting with others, finding support, and leading your life with a strong team, which is essential to transforming your life and achieving your goals.

The Martyr

The light side of the martyr will give of herself for the betterment of others, but many people become martyrs in life when this level of sacrifice is unnecessary. Even though you may know on a logical level that people experience challenges similar to yours, the archetype of the martyr has a tendency to rear its ugly head and keep you in misery. The shadow side of the martyr archetype sends the message that you have to go it alone—nobody understands you. If a cord of wood needs to be stacked, you have to do it all yourself. If you need a new job, you have to work hard to get the interview. The martyr is too full of pride to appreciate the fact that a referral from a friend is how the universe works, and that networking is actually responsible for 80–85 percent of the jobs people acquire.

The martyr will plunk herself down on the couch on a Friday night, convinced that her soul mate must have died in a car accident years ago, which is why she never meets him (or her) when she goes out. The martyr will prevent you from asserting yourself and asking that person you've just been talking to for half an hour if they'd like to meet for a drink sometime, because *if you were worthy, they would have asked you.* She loves it when you're passive-aggressive, because, hey, why bother? Nobody's going to listen to you anyway. She keeps you from charging what you're worth or negotiating the best salary. She tries to convince you that health and fitness are things of the past, or for those who are younger or who have more time to work out. It's too late for you to go after that dream job or learn how to play piano. Give it up. Throw in the towel. Sacrifice your happiness for the greater good, because it's a zero-sum game. There's only so much happiness to go around, and the more you take up, the less there is for others. Besides, your family needs you to stay right where you are. There's no way out.

As a single parent, I have been determined to live a good life in spite of the fact that I'm raising children without the benefit of a partner. I recently had to acknowledge that I've been a bit of a martyr when it comes to admitting I need help and asking for it. I don't quite understand why it is that women will take up collections and coordinate meal plans when a man's wife is ill or out of town, but a woman can raise an entire brood by herself and not one person will offer to help. I once dated a man whose neighbor brought him lunch on a daily basis.

A woman I know put it this way. She was complaining because her husband was away on business, leaving her alone with their three children. On trash day, she had to drag the barrels to the street, which was normally his job.

"Welcome to my world," I laughed.

"Yeah, but you're used to it," she said.

I wanted to smack her.

I finally had to acknowledge that sometimes you have to come right out and tell people you need assistance. When a friend of mine offered to do some home repairs, I can't tell you how happy this made me. I'd done a lot for him and expected nothing in return, but this was his way of repaying the kindness. I later asked him to paint my son's bedroom, which was something I never would have considered doing before. He did, and taught my boys how to do it in the process.

Phil Connors was in many ways a martyr, although for an unknown cause. The reason for his being trapped in Punxatawney, Pennsylvania, on Groundhog Day are unclear, but he embraces it and uses it as an opportunity to better people's lives.

The Hermit

The traditional hermit lives alone to develop an inner life. A certain amount of alone time is good for all of us, but the negative aspect of the hermit is isolation. Your inner martyr's best friend is the hermit, which is ironic, since the shadow side of the hermit tends to fear others, preferring his solitude. But if anybody is going to visit the hermit, it's the martyr, because misery loves company, at least in short spurts. The problem with their friendship is the fact that they tend to reinforce each other's false perceptions that going it alone, doing it "my way," as Frank Sinatra sang, or being the maverick is always best. Rugged individualism has its place, but not here—not when you feel stuck or you're ready to move forward and know that your advancement will require teamwork. The shadow aspects of the martyr and hermit will hold you back. Struggle will become your way of life as you try to force things to happen all by yourself. That's if he doesn't first succeed in getting you to plunk yourself down on the side of the yellow brick road, throw your hands up in despair, and sing, "Some Day My Prince Will Come."

All of the princess stories contain some aspect of isolation, if not in outright solitude, then in the fact that they were hidden—a metaphor for concealing their spirits. Rapunzel was trapped in a castle, Sleeping Beauty was raised in the woods under a false name, Cinderella was locked in her bedroom, and Snow White hid out with seven dwarves. All of them were oppressed, and often by people who should have been there to support them, as we saw with Snow White's stepmother, the Wicked Queen, and Cinderella's evil stepmother and stepsisters. But even these princesses succeeded in finding support. Cinderella had her mice and fairy godmother; Snow White her seven dwarves; Princess Aurora her benevolent fairies; and Rapunzel—well, maybe not Rapunzel. Rapunzel was very selective when it came to letting down her golden hair. At least in *Pretty Woman*, Vivian had her best friend, Kit.

As you may have guessed, your martyr and hermit are good buddies with your inner film critic. They love to talk about your inner film director behind her back.

Beware of characters and temporary situations which will crop up on your way to achieving your goals and dreams.

The God/Goddess

Sitting alongside your inner film director is the light side of your inner god or goddess.

Unlike the princess, a goddess has power. She doesn't relinquish her ruby slippers to please anyone. Think of Aphrodite, the Greek goddess of love and passion. She helps men and women to experience more passion and to balance male/female energy. Kuan Yin, the eastern goddess, helps you feel compassion and mercy towards yourself and others. The Greek goddess Athena teaches you to trust your inner wisdom. As the "warrior goddess" she battles with her wit instead of weapons.

Becoming overly self-indulgent or taking advantage of people is a sign you've moved into the shadow side of the goddess. (p. 28 Guidebook for the Goddess Guidance Oracle Cards, Doreen Virtue)

Like the goddess, the god archetype has the power to be kind and compassionate, but on the shadow side, s/he's a self-indulgent, self-serving dictator.

Phil discovered his god-like powers when, by repeating the same day, he was able to study it and to notice things most of us would ignore. Because everything was the same, it became predictable, and therefore, like a god, he could control the outcome. You can view the scene where he tells Rita he's a god in your Star Pack.

The comedy *Bruce Almighty* starring Jim Cary is another film where the main character is given god's power in order to learn some important life lessons.

The Lover

The light side of the lover archetype extends herself to others, produces quality work, and puts her heart into everything she does, because she cares. She loves people, loves being creative, and loves life. For that reason, her work has value, and she knows it. She's confident about what she produces, because she knows she has a purpose. There's a reason for her being. She pours love into her relationships and her creativity. The positive traits of the princesses were their loving, sweet natures. They loved nature, animals, people, and romance. If we were to identify their primary archetypes, for sure the lover would be one of them.

The lover who becomes infatuated with something or someone or who allows their passion to become obsessive to the point of being self-destructive is operating on the shadow side of this archetype.

Phil certainly went from being a shallow person to a true lover by the end of this film.

The Liberator

The god/goddess and lover love to team up with the liberator, who is here to free you from the self-doubt that keeps you stuck, oppressive beliefs that keep you trapped in your situation, and bad habits such as procrastination, laziness, poor diet, or excuses. The liberator frees you from self-imposed constraints, including the sabotaging thoughts of your inner film critic. She is here to give you the courage to go against convention and break free from naysayers and critics. In step nine, *Edit Your Film*, you'll have an opportunity to see how Micky Ward, the protagonist in the movie *The Fighter*, had to assess the people in his life and determine who was truly providing him with the support he needed to succeed as a prizefighter. This involved finding the incredible courage to break free from relationships that held him back.

Where most transformations of characters involve going from bad to good, an exception may be the Walter White character in the television series *Breaking Bad*. Walter actually transforms in the reverse. An interesting twist, but his character growth happens as a result of liberating himself from fifty years of always trying to do the right thing and never seeming to benefit. After a cancer diagnosis, he breaks the law by making methamphetamine, committing murder, and over a short period of time, becoming a complete bad ass. By liberating himself from society's rules, he goes from weak to strong, unconscious to aware. What's interesting is that in breaking free from his self-imposed chains, he winds up stepping into the shadow aspect of the liberator, which wreaks havoc in other people's lives.

In *Groundhog Day*, Phil liberates himself from his beliefs that he was destined to a life of solitude, undeserving of a woman like Rita. He frees himself from the idea that he didn't need personal connections. By changing his beliefs, he is liberated from the pain of repeating the same day over and over again. Ironically, before the time trap, that's exactly what he'd been doing anyway. It was by literally repeating the same day that he was able to get unstuck.

Like Dorothy, who found her supporting players in her dream as the tin man, scarecrow, and lion, you need to find your inner team—your inner liberator, lover, and goddess, and embrace the light aspects of the martyr and hermit.

Your inner support team constitutes your thoughts. If you are in healthy alignment throughout your chakras, you are in a better position to attract the right people and situations. Instead of attracting people and things to fill a void, you can attract people and things to complement your life. Instead of unfulfilling work, you'll naturally draw to you the work you were meant to do. Same goes for your home life and physical self.

Your outer team will tend to reflect your inner team—much like your movie's antagonist tends to be an outward manifestation of your inner film critic. You begin moving into the realm of your sixth chakra. We'll explore this along with the law of attraction in the next chapter, *Set the Stage, Lead with Vision.*

I'm sure I don't need to tell you who your supporting players are. It doesn't matter if they are sisters and brothers, close cousins, good friends, coworkers, or people in your professional network, as long as they *support* you. Be selective. Just because someone is a relative, it doesn't mean they're going to appreciate you, cheer you on, or encourage you. In fact, they could do just the opposite, so it's important that you evaluate each person and determine whom you want in your close circle.

In addition to the people who surround you naturally, look at the different areas of your life to see where you may want to hire professional support, just as Prince Albert had to find a speech coach. For example, in my business I have a virtual assistant, an attorney, a CPA, a graphic designer, and a web developer. I've also worked with professional mentors and coaches. I am a yoga teacher, but I've benefitted from some great personal trainers in the past, as well as nutritionists for my health.

A friend of mine is a professional organizer who provides support to people who need to find more structure in their business and home environment. As an author, speaker, and coach, I'm playing the supporting role in my client's lives.

Don't overlook areas where you can provide support to others. What skills and talents do you have that could enrich people's lives?

Phil tunes into the light side of his inner lover (pouring love into the community, and ultimately Rita), god (by using his powers to help those in need), liberator (freeing his mind of self-limiting beliefs that told him he wasn't deserving of true love), hermit (developing an inner life), and martyr (giving of himself for the betterment of others).

And that is the true message of the film. If you want to stop repeating the same day over and over again; if you want to wake up to a new day, transform your life, overcome your challenge, and find your act 3 resolution, then you must connect with your courage, mind, and heart. And a big part of that means connecting with others—finding your supporting players.

Phil Connors may not have been a "fan of his fellow man" at the beginning, but he sure came to need them at the end. By understanding that, he wins the heart of Rita. He is freed from having to repeat Groundhog Day. Phil becomes a better version of himself.

Phil's Transformation

ACT 2

Mind
I don't have to go it alone.
I'm worthy of love

Courage
Find significance in each
day. Be vulnerable

Heart
Help others.
I love Rita

ACT 1

ACT 3

Challenge:
Career Stagnation,
Time Trap

Resolution:
Friendship,
Love,
Wakes up to a new day

Summary

As a business owner, I could not do what I do without my team. Anyone who starts a business on a shoestring budget knows that they have to start out doing a lot of the work themselves. Over time, however, if they want their business to grow, they need to delegate certain tasks to other people so that they can focus on what brought them to their business in the first place. Think of the most successful entrepreneurs and all the people they have around them to help—their spouses, assistants, mentors, and other professionals. They need friends to help them through the good times and the bad in business and in their personal lives as well.

To find support, join a networking club, and try on-line dating if you're looking for love. If you are in a career or have your own business that would benefit from mutual connections around a particular topic, starting your own group is a great idea. Tell your connections that you're interested in joining groups in your area of interest. It's quite possible a group already exists on Facebook or LinkedIn. Send friend requests to people you interact with regularly. I recently formed my own mastermind group. I meet with three other women twice a month by phone. We discuss our latest projects, give each other ideas, and help keep one another accountable. Don't underestimate the value of live, in-person networking. Social media is a great way to meet new people, but it cannot replace the value of face-to-face. I think people today are becoming a bit lost in cyberspace. Internet connection has its benefits, but it's nothing compared to live interaction.

Be mindful of when the shadow side of the martyr and hermit appear in your life and try to keep you stuck in a victim-like state of isolation. Remember how Phil Connors transformed his life by connecting with the light aspects of these archetypes, as well as his inner lover, god, and liberator. Reach out to others who may need your support, and watch what comes back to you in return. Remember, a key to effective networking isn't to go into it thinking WIIFM (What's In It For Me?) but about what *you* have to offer.

This is one of the keys to transforming your life. There's no magic formula or ideal number of people to connect with. Tune in to your inner film director for guidance. She'll help point you in the right direction for finding your team.

Notes

STEP EIGHT

Set the Stage

Lead with Vision

Willie Wonka and the Chocolate Factory

Int. Chocolate Factory

The parents and children are licking the wallpaper, which is covered in a fruit pattern.

        Willie Wonka
  Try some more. The strawberries taste
    like strawberries. The snosberries
         taste like snosberries.

         Veruca Salt
  Snosberries? Whoever heard of a snosberry?

        Willie Wonka
  We are the music makers, and we
    are the dreamers of dreams.

Willy Wonka and the Chocolate Factory

On the opening scene of *Willy Wonka and the Chocolate Factory*, the children from Charlie Bucket's (Peter Ostrum) school go to Bill's Candy Shoppe for a treat, but Charlie has no money. He lives with his mother (Diana Sowle), a widow who earns a living doing other people's laundry. She also takes care of Charlie's bedridden grandparents. It's a bit odd that the four of them haven't been out of bed in twenty years—and they all share the same one—but it is part of what makes this film quirky and fun. Charlie shares a close bond with his Grandpa Joe (Jack Albertson).

Willy Wonka (Gene Wilder), a local candy maker, hasn't allowed anyone to set foot in his chocolate factory in years, but he announces that he's hidden five golden tickets in his Wonka Bars. The lucky ones who find them will get to tour his factory, and the "winner" will receive a lifetime supply of chocolate. "Wonkamania" becomes a global obsession.

The first to win is Augustus Gloop, a gluttonous German boy, followed by Veruca Salt, a spoiled English girl whose father has all of his employees search through boxes upon boxes of chocolate bars to find a golden ticket. As each ticket is found, Charlie grows more disheartened. He tells his mother that he wants it more than anybody. She sings, "Cheer Up, Charlie."

Violet Beauregarde, a gum-chewing American girl, is the next to win, followed by Mike Teavee, a boy who can't keep his eyes off the television.

Charlie's hopes are dashed when news breaks that the final ticket has been found by a gambler from Paraguay.

The next day, when a sad Charlie leaves school, he finds a gold coin in a sewer grate outside of Bill's Candy Shoppe. He decides to buy a Wonka Scrumdidlyumptious, and after gobbling it down, buys a second Wonka bar to bring home to Grandpa Joe. On the street, everyone is scrambling to buy a newspaper. It turns out that the man from Paraguay was a fraud, and there's still one ticket left. Charlie unwraps his chocolate bar and finds the golden ticket inside.

Each of the children, including Charlie, is approached by Slugworth, Wonka's competition, who asks them to steal candy from the factory so he can copy it.

Grandpa Joe musters the strength to get out of bed so that he can accompany Charlie on his tour of the factory. The next day, the children arrive with one of their parents, and the eccentric Wonka shows up wearing a brown top hat and a purple coat, and carrying a cane. The Wonka Chocolate Factory is a magical place full of fun rooms and tiny doors. The first room they enter is entirely edible. Wonka sings "Pure Imagination" as everyone runs to taste all the candy. They discover that Wonka's factory workers are tiny men with green hair and orange faces called Oompa Loompas.

Against Wonka's directive not to contaminate the chocolate river, Augustus drinks from it, falls in, gets sucked through a chocolate extraction pipe, and is sent to the Fudge Room.

In the Inventing Room, the children are given an Everlasting Gob-stopper, the candy Slugworth asked each of them to steal. Like Augustus, Violet refuses to listen to Wonka and tries some gum that is still in the experimental stage. She blows up into a giant blueberry and is taken by one of the Oompa Loompa's to the juicing room to be squeezed.

Charlie and Grandpa Joe stay behind in the Bubble Room to try the Fizzy Lifting Drink. They begin floating and have a great time until they come close to getting sucked into a ceiling fan. Grandpa Joe discovers that burping sends them back down to the ground.

After setting her eyes on the giant geese that lay golden Easter eggs, Veruca Salt insists that she have one for herself and sings "I Want it Now." The brat stands on the Eggometer, which labels her a "bad egg" and sends her down a chute to the Chocolate Golden Egg Sorting Room. Charlie and Mike Teevee are the only children left. Wonka introduces them to his new invention, Wonkavision, a broadcasting technology that can send objects through television instead of pictures. Like all the other children, Mike doesn't listen to Wonka, sends himself through, and winds up only a few inches tall. His mother puts him in her purse and is escorted to a place where he can be stretched back to size.

Charlie is the last child still on the tour. Wonka abruptly shows them the way out and enters his office, closing the door behind him. Grandpa Joe sticks up for Charlie and opens Wonka's door to find that everything in the room is cut in half—half-clocks, half-desks, half-everything. He asks about Charlie's lifetime supply of chocolate. Wonka shouts at them, saying that Charlie violated his contract by sampling the Fizzy Lifting Drink, making his prize null and void. Grandpa Joe vows revenge, but Charlie turns around, slowly walks toward Wonka, and places the Gobstopper on his desk.

Wonka places his hand on the piece of candy, recants, and asks them for forgiveness. He reveals that Slugworth is actually an employee named Wilkinson, and it was part of a test. He tells Charlie, "You won!"

Wonka leads Charlie and Grandpa Joe to the Wonkavator, a multi-dimensional glass elevator. They fly up and out of the factory, and Wonka tells Charlie that his actual prize is the entire factory. As he puts it, he cannot run the factory forever, and he can't hand it over to an adult because they'll want to do everything their own way. He needed to pass it down to a child. Charlie finds out that he and his entire family can move into the factory. He has won the ultimate prize.

Set the Stage
Lead with Vision

*P*erhaps you think it odd that I should choose a children's movie for this step, but I couldn't think of anything more appropriate. Either that or I'm just immature, but I don't think so. Because to set the stage for your ideal life, you need to use your imagination, as Charlie Bucket and Willie Wonka do in this film. Imagination comes easy to children, so to revisit a children's story—about a fantastical chocolate factory with Oompa Loompas and a successful businessman wearing a purple coat and a top hat—well, it's just perfect.

When you think about it, before they are corrupted by adults and the limitations we place on them, children have wild imaginations. If you ask them what they want to be when they grow up, they think nothing of telling you a ballerina, a model, a basketball star, or a superhero. It never occurs to them that they can't, and when they're little, we indulge them. My niece, Leah, used to love wearing her Snow White costume every day. Another little boy I knew was Superman on a regular basis. They lived in a world of pure imagination. It's a bit of a shame that somewhere along the way we teach them to be practical. Shedding the costumes is probably a good idea, but not letting go of the idea of possibility.

Remember when you were a child and you thought you could be any-thing? At some point, you were probably told to be realistic, and so you scaled back your goals and dreams to something more socially acceptable, or something your family felt was practical. Isn't it odd that people find pro-fessions like nursing or teaching to be realistic and achievable, yet a desire to

> *"Imagination is everything. It is the preview of life's coming attractions. Imagination is more important than knowledge."*
>
> *—Albert Einstein*

act or sing causes our biggest supporters to shrink in horror because we'll only wind up disappointed. *There's just no way you can succeed, not with all that competition.* This is especially true for any creative endeavor, whether it's music, art, writing, or the like. It brings out everyone's inner film critic. There's something very exposing about creativity. I'd almost rather bump into a co-worker on a nude beach than hear them read my work aloud.

Even a portfolio career—one in which you earn multiple streams of income from a variety of professions, seems radical and risky to some. But the thing people don't understand is that on the path toward your goal, you will be introduced to so many new things, that you may discover something even better than what you had originally imagined.

My son, Jack has been told by some of his friends that his dream to become a film director is impossible. Yet if you could see what he's taught himself to do in the five years since he saved up his money to buy his first camera, you could absolutely see how it's possible. He was born an artist. I believe in him, but as he gets older, he has to deal with these naysayers. That's why I chose Willie Wonka and the Chocolate Factory. It is the perfect metaphor for how you can harness the law of attraction to set the stage for your ideal life. Not only do you have a strong character serving as the protagonist, Charlie Bucket, but a quirky man running a chocolate factory who never lost his childlike imagination and sense of play. As Wonka says, "We are the music makers, and we are the dreamers of dreams."

It's time to embrace your inner child again. It's time to start dreaming. Your dreams can't come true if you don't have any. Your imagination is your golden ticket to your desired future. The key is to make sure that what you envision is *your* vision, not what society, your family, or even the standards of success defined in your career field say you're supposed to want for your life.

Like Charlie and Willie Wonka, you will use your imagination and apply the principles of the law of attraction to achieve your heart's desire. But before I go on, I must admit that there are some things about the law of attraction make me roll my eyes. Even though I'm writing about it, there's a part of me that's still a skeptic. Maybe it's my inner film critic talking, but maybe not. Movies like *The Secret* made it sound as though all you have to do is sit and think real hard about what you want and *really* believe it, and it'll show up at your door. And if you don't get it, then it's your fault, because you attract everything. Are we really to believe that we have that much power and control? Are we to look at people living in third world countries and attribute scarcity of food and water to the fact that they haven't attracted it? I'm sure the law of attraction experts have an explanation for this, but I have never been able to wrap my brain around it.

While I do believe in the con-

> *"Those who believe that they can achieve the object of their Definite Chief Aim do not recognize the word impossible. Neither do they acknowledge a temporary defeat. They know they are going to succeed, and if one plan fails they quickly replace it with another plan."*
>
> *—The Secret Law of Attraction as Explained by Napoleon Hill*

cepts of the law of attraction, a big part of me thinks that it's become something that can make a person feel bad for not being, doing, and having everything they want. I believe that there's an aspect of divine timing at play, and there are many things we don't have a say in. But, I do believe we play a big part in creating our lives. Of course we do.

In this step you'll have an opportunity to examine your relationship to some more archetypes that you may want to connect with in order to manifest your ideal life, and you'll review the sixth—or third eye—chakra, your center of intuitive insight, an essential quality you need to learn how to access and trust in order to succeed in setting the stage for your life story.

Storyteller

Remember back when you first started this process? The first step, *Embrace Your Inner Screenwriter*, introduced you to the concept that you are the writer of your own life story. You don't have full control over the events of your life, but you do have the ability to write a script, as you go, that empowers you to move forward with faith instead of remaining stuck (because of fear) in your act 1 challenge. You have tapped into the light side of your storyteller archetype and started writing the story based on how you'd like your movie's third act to turn out. Throughout, you've also been paying attention to those two inner voices: the voice of your inner film critic and the voice of your inner film director. Each of these voices has a story to tell, but it's up to you whose script you'll follow.

For some, the storyteller is a primary archetype that manifests itself in a professional writing or speaking career. But we all have the stories we tell ourselves. Your shadow storyteller may stretch or hide truth. When you're not ready to make a change, your inner storyteller may make up a story that will allow you to live in denial for a while longer. But the light side of your storyteller will help you to not only write a fact-based story, but one that includes an even better version of your life. Your storyteller uses your imagination and intuitive insight to create your life, much as Willie Wonka used it to invent new candies. Even though Charlie Bucket is growing up in poverty and billions of people worldwide are all searching, he believes he can be one of the five who finds a golden ticket. The story he tells himself is one where it is possible, in spite of the fact that his family can't afford to buy caseloads of candy bars to increase his odds for winning. He only opens two bars. As he tells his mother, he

> *"The great artists, writers, musicians, and poets become great because they acquire the habit of relying upon the "still small voice" that speaks from within, through their creative imagination. Anyone with a keen imagination knows that some of their best ideas come through so-called "hunches."*
>
> —*The Secret Law of Attraction as Explained by Napoleon Hill*

"wants it more than anybody." His belief is so strong that it even manifests a gold coin lying in the storm drain. Even though he thinks that all of the golden tickets have been found, he still uses the money to buy a candy bar, and then another. He said it was to take home to Grandpa Joe, but the look on his face says that something inside is nudging him to buy one more bar. When he finds out the man from Paraguay is a fake, it's as if he *knows* that golden ticket is inside his bar. (You can view the scene where Charlie finds the golden ticket in your Star Pack).

Can you think of a time when something inside nudged you to do something nonsensical, or when everyone told you it was too late or impossible, but it turned out to be the best thing you could have done? Or maybe you didn't listen and later regretted it.

The demon of the fifth chakra is lies. The lies we tell ourselves interfere with our ability to build the life we truly want. As you create your life story, ask yourself whether or not this is *your* story, or a story you think you're supposed to be writing for your life, based on someone else's expectations. If the dream isn't yours, then it'll be next to impossible to achieve, or if you do, hard to enjoy. It's not what you want.

Although this movie is a work of fiction, you can look at Charlie's golden ticket as a metaphor, an example of what it means to believe, take action, envision, and allow. Like Charlie, make sure you take time to consider what you truly want. Do you really need a million dollars, or is it that you just want to be happy and decided somewhere along the way that being rich would make you happy? Do you want to be a famous artist, or is it that you think fame is the only way of justifying the time and money you spend making art? Maybe what you truly want is to be more at peace with your investments and less concerned with what other people think.

You have been going through the steps of making your movie. You've been working on your script, becoming a better producer, developing your character, listening to the wisdom of your inner director, and recognizing when your inner film critic is trying to sabotage your progress. You've taken center stage as a star; you're learning your lines, and finding supporting players. Now it's time to set the stage. This step is where you design the set, choose your film score, select your costume, and if you're single, imagine your ideal costar—your leading lady or man. You hold the golden ticket.

When you imagine a future—when you say to the universe, *this is what I desire,* and you do your part to create it, the universe will meet you halfway. The future will draw you to it like a magnet. Sound impossible? I don't think it is, even though, as I said, I am a skeptic. I know that before I began writing, I imagined a finished book. I don't think I could have ever completed one if I couldn't picture it in my mind. The same holds true for finding my house and creating the kind of home environment I wanted to raise my boys in. If you look around you and think about your life, I'm sure you can see how you've created a life based on what you've imagined and believed was possible. And I don't mean that you can ever achieve perfection. But you can take what you've got, make the best of it, and continue rewriting the script that keeps you working toward a goal.

The Visionary

Your visionary is going to help you to envision a future that you may, up until now, have only thought possible for other, or special, people. A true visionary is able to see possibilities and tap into her courage to do things that are true to that vision, rather than staying stuck in only seeing what has been in the past, as if that were a predictor of the future. Willie Wonka is absolutely a visionary. His factory is a result of his vision. In your Star Pack you'll have access the scene where he sings "Pure Imagination." I love the lyrics:

> *Come with me, And you'll be*
> *In a world of pure imagination*
> *Take a look and you'll see*
> *Into your imagination.*
> *We'll begin with a spin*
> *Traveling in the world of my creation*
> *What we'll see will defy explanation.*

Charlie is also a visionary. He sees himself winning. When I think of visionaries, I think of people like Steve Jobs of Apple, Inc., or film directors such as James Cameron or Steven Spielberg.

Beware of the shadow side of the visionary, who will want to censor your vision. That shadow side will want you to conform to someone else's vision to make it more comfortable or acceptable to him or her. Your inner director will work alongside the light side of your visionary.

The Magical Child

As you create your vision, ask your inner magical child to play with you. Your magical child will help you be as playful and imaginative as possible. She's going to view the world from a perspective that you, as an adult, may be quick to brush off as silly or unrealistic. The parents in *Willie Wonka* had completely lost touch with their magical child. That shadow side will pull your character back into a world of depression, pessimism, or disbelief. Remember your diet of the mind and shut out this voice of your inner film critic. Allow your magical child to have a field day full of creativity.

Willie Wonka is the magical child personified. Grandpa Joe and Charlie have no trouble accessing this aspect of themselves as well. The entire chocolate factory— a room that is entirely edible, a chocolate river, flavored wallpaper, and the contest to find a child to inherit his factory—is a result of Wonka's imagination and playfulness. Phil Connors from *Groundhog Day* is also a big, magical child. I love the scene where he and Rita make a snow man and get into a snowball fight with some local children. J. K. Rowling, author of the Harry Potter books, certainly had to access her magical child to create those stories, particularly the "magic" piece. Einstein strikes me as someone who must have been quite playful. Other magical children include comedians such as Jim Carrey, Robin Williams, and one of my favorite comedic actresses, Sophia Vergara.

The Fool

"I don't want to make a fool of myself."

How often does that fear keep you from acting? I'm incredibly afraid of making a fool of myself, but I know it's just a fear. It isn't real, not that it's never happened before. I don't even want to think about it. But in this case, I would encourage you to allow your character to be foolish, only in a good way. The light side of the fool is a character who allows him or herself to be a bit silly in order to explore life without regard for what other people may think. Just beware of the shadow side of the fool who may put on a mask, like a clown, and use humor in order to cover emotional hurt (like Phil Connors). Ask your playful fool to help you to break free of anything holding you back. It's okay to be silly.

Willie Wonka, in his top hat and purple coat, doesn't mind playing the fool. He is silly, and he doesn't care what any of the parents think of him or his wacky ideas. He allows their snide remarks to roll right off his back and at times gives it right back to them. It's like he knows something they don't, and judging by his success, we suspect he does.

Whenever I think of someone who lived on the light side of the fool archetype, I think of Lucille Ball. Her willingness to be foolish created one of the most beloved and hilarious sitcoms of the fifties, *I Love Lucy*. Since we're on the subject of chocolate, I've included a famous scene where she and Ethel work in a chocolate factory in your Star Pack. Feel free to take a break to go watch it.

In the 2005 remake starring Johnny Depp as Willie Wonka, we got to see a touch of the shadow side of the fool when his character reveals that a lot of his quirkiness stems from issues he has with his parents. I think that's why I didn't like this version as much as the original. It wasn't that I didn't like Johnny Depp's interpretation, it was that I didn't like the fact that his character was made to appear screwed up for being so eccentric and imaginative. I like the idea that Wonka's eccentricity and childlike imagination are perfectly normal and beneficial, because these are the qualities that allow him to create such a wonderful place. I loved viewing a character who is silly for the sake of silliness; a man who is a bit foolish and childlike because it allows him to create a successful business, not because of some childhood wound. (The original also had better Oompa Loompas, plus it was a musical. What's *Willie Wonka and the Chocolate Factory* without the Oompa Loompas singing "Oompa, Loompa, Doompaty, Doo"?) The transformation was for Charlie to experience, not Wonka. Wonka is a great example of what it means to be a successful entrepreneur, because he can imagine and play.

The Pioneer

If you're like me, images of women from the eighteen-hundreds wearing long, drab, brown, heavy dresses with their hair tied back in buns, and men with thick moustaches carrying hunting rifles come to mind when I think of the pioneer. To me, the pioneer is synonymous with going west during the California Gold Rush or to the frontier to claim new land. These were people who took tremendous risks in order to build a better life. They faced amazing antagonists—hostile Indians, severe weather, illness, injury, hardships—but they did it anyway.

Is your vision something that seems outlandish or risky to more "reasonable" people? Are you doing something that's completely new to you, with an outcome that's unknown? Good! Perhaps you need to embrace the light side of the pioneer and dare to live a life that others are too afraid to try. Go against convention. Be a risk taker. Do things you have never thought were possible. Find solutions to whatever challenges present themselves along the way. Remember your ruby slippers and stay in your personal power. Be like the men and women from the pioneer days, braving the American frontier and crossing the country. Just be aware of your pioneer's shadow, who may want to jump from one thing to the next—always trying something new but never sticking to something long enough to see results.

The Gambler

Employ a little bit of the gambler. No, I don't want you to risk your life savings or quit your job without having something else lined up, or like Violet chewing gum before it's ready, or Mike Teevee sending himself through Wonkavision. That would be unwise. But the light side of the gambler will allow you to go with your gut and follow your intuitive hunches about something, like Charlie when he buys the second candy bar—the one that has the golden ticket inside. An entrepreneur must be a visionary, a pioneer, and a gambler. Think of people like Warren Buffet, whose career involves many large-scale investments. The word gambler may have a negative connotation, but looked at archetypically, a gambler is simply a person who takes risks based on weighing the odds and following their instincts.

Just don't fall under the illusion that you don't have to take action and do the work required to achieve your vision, like the man from

Paraguay who claimed he found the last golden ticket. Don't confuse the light side of the gambler with a cheat.

Sixth Chakra: Third Eye

I have to say that out of all of the chakras, this has to be one of my favorites, because I love this topic—intuition. The third eye chakra is located around the forehead. Its color is indigo, and its element is *light*. It connects to your brain, nervous system, eyes, ears, nose, and pineal and pituitary glands. It pertains to intuition, imagination, and psychic insight. Its demon is *illusion*.

Do you think you're intuitive? I've often had people tell me that they're not, but that's not possible. We're all intuitive. It's how we're made. The trouble is that your intuition often tells you things you don't want to hear. It may guide you to do things that will mean major change and upheaval in your life, like leaving a job or ending a relationship. But the less you listen, the more out of alignment in your body you become. Your energetic system will tell you if you're not heeding your own inner director's guidance through discomfort or even illness.

For example, your intuition may tell you a particular person or situation isn't good for you, and it's time to move on. Refusing to listen and staying stuck may show up as foot or leg pain. Your intuition says that you need to do something creative, or get your finances in order, but if you allow your inner critic to sabotage you and stand in your way, it could result in issues in your second chakra, or reproductive area. Your intuition may tell you to stand up for yourself and not allow another person to squash your dreams. If you do the opposite, your stomach or intestines may be the first part of your system to object. If you're not being kind to yourself or connecting to heart wisdom, you'll feel it in that area of your body.

Notice if you're clearing your throat a lot or getting choked up—it may be a sign that your intuition is telling you to speak up, but you're allowing your fears to keep you silent. Your body is an excellent way to tap into your intuitive source. I found depression and anxiety to be my body's way of telling me to pay more attention to my intuition. Recently, it was a sign that I cannot work alone all the time. I need people around me. When I answered the door at eleven o'clock in the morning on weekday, still in my pajamas, I knew it was time to go back to the office. What's your body telling you?

> "Concentrate your mind on the attainment of the object of a deeply seated desire, and soon you will attract, through those forces that no one can explain, the material counterparts of that desire."
>
> —The Secret Law of Attraction

Intuition—inner vision and your ability to imagine are connected. In order to connect, you have to be able to tap into the various sources of intuitive insight.

One way is through dreams. Getting back to our core movie, Oz is Dorothy's dream world. Your dreams can be an excellent indicator of what you need to pay more attention to in your waking life. Your dreams also speak in metaphor and symbolism, just as Oz is full of symbolism and metaphor. When I was looking for a new place to live, I had a dream that I threw my air conditioner out the window of my car. It got increasingly hotter until I came to a fork in the road. A sign for Wrentham appeared. Symbolically, throwing my AC out the window and getting hotter was a metaphor for the expression "you're getting warmer," like the childhood game when you're trying to guess the right answer and your friend tells you when you're getting close. In the dream I got a literal sign, which is rare. I now live in Wrentham.

Your dreams can provide excellent clues, but your active imagination can also help in creating your reality. This is where the law of attraction comes into play. Until you can bring your imagination into alignment with your belief about what is possible for your life, and you are willing to take the steps necessary to create it, nothing will happen. But again, it has to be your vision and your beliefs, not those that you think you're supposed to have. I fell into this trap myself. I share my story at the end of this chapter.

Another way to tap into your intuition is through signs in your waking life. Notice if you wake up with a particular song playing in your head, what you're drawn to in the bookstore, or what jumps out at you in other areas of your life. Like Charlie when he notices a gold coin lying in the storm drain, your intuition is at work, telling you to pay attention.

Keep a dream journal and record your dreams right after you wake up. Contemplate their meaning.

Keep a regular journal. I get up most mornings and write three pages in a notebook to tap into anything that's bothering me or simply record my thoughts. (Some of it probably makes me sound crazy, so if I'm ever in an accident, please assure my family I was just venting. I didn't mean all of it.)

Meditate. Keep it simple—sit in a chair and close your eyes for fifteen minutes. When I'm writing, I do this regularly, because I have to quiet my mind chatter so that the words that I want can come through. Most of my writing is done up in my head before it hits the paper. I also love a walking meditation. I get my best ideas when I go for a walk.

Notice your eating and exercise habits. Are you foraging in the cabinets, stuffing your feelings to avoid an uncomfortable truth? Are you starving yourself because you feel like your life is out of control? Are you over-exercising, and if so, what feelings are you running away from? Are you avoiding it altogether, and if so, how does that make you feel?

Remember to embrace the archetypes that will help you to develop psychic insight: your visionary, magical child, fool, pioneer, and gambler. These characters are intuitive and insightful. And keep in mind that all of this requires an act of surrender. Remember when the witch painted the word surrender across the sky? It wasn't just about giving up Dorothy to the witch or giving away her ruby slippers, it was about releasing your inner control freak and surrendering to the divine, your ultimate source of inspiration. Contrary to what law of attraction experts say, you are not in control of everything. This becomes quite obvious when you have kids. You may influence the actions and behaviors of others, but they are not your puppets. I actually find comfort in this. Focusing on what's within your control and letting go of what isn't is incredibly empowering, not to mention efficient.

Keep in mind that thoughts are things. They create your reality. Keep tapping into the voice of your inner film director. Like attracts like, so the more you focus on already having what you want, the more likely it will manifest in your life.

Beware of illusion, the demon of the sixth chakra. The voice of illusion is the one that tells you you're unworthy and that what you want isn't possible to achieve. These can become self-fulfilling prophesies. Like my son Jack, you need to be aware of when you are sabotaging yourself.

I became a yoga teacher in 1999. I absolutely loved it—studying it, practicing it, and teaching it. Like anything, a certain image comes to mind when you think of a yoga teacher. Chances are you imagine a thin vegetarian who spends most of her time in meditation. She doesn't get angry, she smells of incense, and closes every email with Namaste. This isn't me. At one point, I was even on the Atkins diet. (I don't recommend it.) A man I knew said that he would only go to a yoga class if it was being taught by what he considered a "real" yoga teacher. To him that meant someone who studied for years under a guru from India and who spent her entire professional life teaching yoga. I had a full-time job that had nothing to do with yoga. The fact that I ate meat, had a curvy body, didn't speak in Sanskrit, and had no desire to go to India had me wondering if I should even be teaching. Was I doing a disservice to my students? Was I a fake? I finally decided this was absurd. I loved it, and I was good at it. Not only that, but yoga is more than a set of physical exercises. It's a philosophy that you practice off the mat which includes acceptance. I had a group of people that came to my class every night for two years until I moved away. That was all the proof I needed. I attracted a following because I had a passion for it, and I did what was required of me to become a yoga teacher. I didn't just wish for it. I completed a 200 hour certification course.

The law of attraction states that everything in your life is something you've attracted. You know how I feel about this. It can't be just a matter of focus, but about all of the steps in this book. Go back to the fourth step, Listen to Your Director, and make sure you're not only using positive affirmations to create your reality, but that you're doing what's required of you to make it happen. If your intuition is telling you that in order to attract something you want, you need to make certain changes first, then you need to make those changes. It's a balance between surrendering, allowing, and doing your part, because just thinking about it won't work. You have to listen to inner guidance. Imagine Glinda, the Good Witch of the North, by your side, going one step at a time along the path to your act 3 resolution.

The movie, *The Secret*, as well as the book it was based on, is about the law of attraction. The movie by Louise Hay, *You Can Heal Your Life*, is about negative versus positive thinking and how to attract wonderful things in your life. The classic book by Napoleon Hill, *Think and Grow Rich* is about using the law of attraction to build wealth. I recommend a book called *The Secret Law of Attraction as Explained by Napoleon Hill*, which summarizes the main concepts in his original book.

Charlie's Transformation

ACT 2

Mind
He can be one in
ten billion

Courage
To believe it's possible
for him

Heart
Pure of heart. Honest.
Gives Gobstopper back.

ACT 1

ACT 3

Challenge:
Poverty.
Wants a golden ticket.

Resolution:
Inherits the chocolate
factory. Lifts family out
of poverty.

Summary

In the eighth step to starring in your own life story, *Set the Stage, Lead with Vision,* you use your imagination and intuition to develop a new vision for your life. Connect with the light side of your visionary, magical child, fool, pioneer, and gambler, and continue scripting your ideal life by fully embracing your inner storyteller. Listen to your inner director and trust your intuition. Listen to your body and notice your environment, dreams, and things that seem like coincidences, as these may be ways your inner wisdom is speaking to you.

Defining Success Your Way

How is success defined in your field?

As the author of a self-help book, it seems that success in this field is defined as a millionaire who has thousands of people on an email list. She has thousands of Twitter followers and Facebook fans, a full coaching practice, and she's a sought-after public speaker. She's successful because she doesn't have to go to a job every day, meaning she doesn't work for someone else.

As I've written this book, I've had to ask myself this question, because I am not a millionaire with thousands of followers. Perhaps it's putting the cart before the horse, but at times I've wondered how I can publish a book about overcoming challenges if I haven't achieved that standard of perfection.

A year ago, I decided to go part-time with my job as a Solutions Consultant at Brainshark to see if I could make a career of writing, speaking and coaching. *Stuck with Mr. Wrong* won four book awards, I'd earned a certificate in coaching many years ago, and I had a lot of experience as a trainer. I thought maybe I was being called to do this. I was told I had a natural coaching program by "experts" in the field. It was a risk. It was a big cut in pay, but I thought it was worth it. I spent 2012 working from home, creating a coaching program, writing this book, and building my web presence, while my main income source was Brainshark. I felt as though my act 1 challenge was to become the success story I defined above.

But something interesting happened along the way. I became depressed. About three or four months into my new work life, I found myself feeling blue, which wasn't like me. Here I was, doing what I thought I loved and finally working from home. I didn't have that long commute anymore. What was the problem?

I realized I missed my co-workers. I missed being in an office. While my colleagues in the coaching field would talk about their escape from corporate life and defined "making it" as no longer having to work a job, I finally came to realize that my personal definition of success wasn't the same. I love contributing to a team. I enjoy the community that's formed in an office environment. I like the friendships, lunch dates, travel, and the ability to contribute to a shared goal. I also love being a positive presence. I'd had the great fortune of working with and for some great people. Where women thirty years ago fought to achieve equality in the workplace, women now were being told that the ultimate achievement was to be able to escape it. We stopped trying to change things for the better.

When messages flooded my inbox about the next how-to-become-a-millionaire-web course or marketing book on how to develop a seven-figure coaching practice, I noticed that instead of feeling excited and inspired, I felt defeated and discouraged. Is this what it's all about?

Book coaches talked about how you don't want to "write the wrong book." In other words, you don't want to make the mistake of writing a book that doesn't further your business.

The artist in me wondered how it was possible to write the wrong book.

Law of attraction experts claimed that if you're not making millions, it's something in your thoughts and beliefs preventing it.

Felt a bit like blame.

I'm not a fan.

A relationship coach wrote about "Single Syndrome" – a made-up illness whose main symptom is having no ring on your finger.

A marketing expert boasted about how she invested over one hundred thousand dollars to learn her trade. The underlying message was that unless you were willing to remortgage your home, you'd never make it.

Everywhere I looked, another coach was promoting a program to people like me, and I started to wonder if the key to making money in this field was to coach coaches and to charge a whole lot of money for it.

I'd spent thousands of dollars on programs that promised so much, but delivered so little. Well-meaning experts asked me why I was "playing it small" before I made the decision to work part-time. The message was that my success in a corporate environment was small, and by default, "big" meant owning my own business. But something didn't feel right. Was it really a "small" thing to make someone happy, brighten someone's day, or help a client find a solution to their problem? Was "big" running a teleclass with thousands of people on the end of the phone?

It took me a while, but I finally figured out that it wasn't my inner critic talking; it was my inner wisdom trying to get my attention. She was telling me that I was allowing myself to get carried away by someone else's definition of success, and by constantly feeling as though I was supposed to be going after this big goal, I wasn't feeling successful now, even though I'd accomplished quite a lot. That's no way to live.

I re-learned something I would tell my clients—if you're passionate about something, it shows. When something's a natural fit, it doesn't feel like struggle. As a yoga teacher, I know this. Our bodies tell us all the time when something's off. Anxiety, depression, back aches, and stiff shoulders don't just come from diet or the fact that your desk isn't ergonomically designed. It's trying to tell you that you're not listening to your intuition and doing what you're meant to do. When your heart and mind aren't in alignment, it shows up in your body.

I'm a hard worker, but if I'm not having fun (at least most of the time), then I know something's off. I was working my tail off for little reward, and much of it wasn't enjoyable. Like forcing yourself to fall in love with someone, it just doesn't work. He may be a great guy who's got everything you're supposed to want, but eventually you have to face it: it's either there or it isn't. Just as attraction can't be forced, you can't force yourself to love a job. I love coaching. I love speaking to groups. I love writing. But I didn't like trying to make my creative life my livelihood, or at least struggling to try to make it my livelihood. Moreover, I didn't have to. While I don't enjoy commuting every day, I also wasn't thriving being at home all the time. I needed to strike a balance. To me, balance was a steady paycheck, teaching yoga a couple times a week, and speaking a few times a month to share my books.

I'm allowing myself to define success my way and allowing it to unfold organically. Success isn't a million dollars. If it is, then the vast majority of us are failures. (Not that I'd turn it away.) For me, success is an eclectic career that balances my love for my job, my role as a parent, teaching yoga, writing, and being as exceptional as possible in all that I do.

None of us walk around thinking, *I'm behaving inauthentically*. But if you feel like a teenager, pressured into the latest trend in athletic shoes and blue jeans, then chances are you're living by another's standards of success and struggling to go after a goal that isn't yours.

Go back and think about how success is defined in your field, and then ask yourself this question.

Is this how I define success, or is this how I think I'm supposed to define success?

If it's the latter, take a breather and figure out what you really, really want. Then do that.

Notes

Notes

STEP NINE

Edit Your Film

Lead with Discernment

The Wizard of Oz

Int. Emerald City

Dorothy, the Tin Man, Scarecrow, and Lion and
are standing before the great and powerful Oz,
hoping he can grant their requests.

> OZ'S VOICE
> The beneficent Oz has every intention
> of granting your request!

> LION
> What's that? What'd he say?

> DOROTHY
> Oh—Oh, come on.

> LION
> Huh? What'd he say?

> OZ'S VOICE
> But first, you must prove yourselves worthy
> by performing a very small task. Bring me
> the broomstick of the Witch of the West.

> TIN MAN
> B-B-B-But if we do that, we'll
> have to kill her to get it!

> OZ'S VOICE
> Bring me her broomstick, and I'll
> grant your requests. Now go!

> LION
> But—but what if she kills us first?

> OZ'S VOICE
> I...said...Go!

The Fighter

Micky Ward is a boxer who dreams of winning a prizefight, but he cannot seem to get ahead. His biggest challenge is his family; his brother, Dicky Eklund (Christian Bale), who was a professional boxer, is his trainer. But he's also a drug addict. Throughout the movie he's the subject of a documentary on meth addiction and at one point goes to jail. As the younger brother of a professional fighter, Micky is kept in the role of student, an archetype we'll explore in this chapter. He's always the underling, never able to graduate beyond the level his brother attained. His mother (Melissa Leo) is his manager, and she reinforces this dynamic. She's extremely controlling and limited in terms of how far she can take his career. In some ways she is the shadow rescuer, another archetype we'll review. She is in denial of the extent of her son's addiction. She is also the smothering mother. All nine of her children are adults, yet she is still very much in charge of their lives, or at least tries to be.

Mickey meets and falls in love with a bartender, Charlene (Amy Adams), who helps him to see that when a new manager offers to take him on, he's being given an opportunity to take his career to a professional level. Micky's biggest act of courage involves firing his brother and his mother as business partners. In order to develop a winner's mindset and fully step into his career, he must edit them out of these roles in his life.

He goes through a transformation like the steps in this book and takes center stage in his life as the lead character. It requires a tremendous amount of courage for him to go against his mother's wishes. He steps out of the shadow student role, takes charge of his career (becomes a producer), develops confidence, loves himself enough to honor his dreams and show tough love to his family, asserts himself, develops a new team, and believes in his vision of winning a prizefight.

Micky eventually invites his brother back as one of his trainers. By the third act, everyone comes together to give him the support he needs to win, and they celebrate his success together. Mickey accepts his "Oscar" as the winner of the fight.

Editing

"The activity of selecting the scenes to be shown and putting them together to create a film. Creating by removal: the act of creating by removing something." (Free Online Dictionary by Farlex.)

Editors, with the guidance of a director, edit film until it meets with the director's approval. It is the art, technique, and practice of assembling shots into a coherent whole."

Edit Your Film
Lead with Discernment

*T*he focus of the ninth step, *Edit Your Film*, is on leading your life with discernment. You'll look at your life through the lens of the movie editor, whose job is to cut unnecessary aspects of the story and to pull everything together into a cohesive whole. Together with your inner film director, you have the power to decide what belongs in your story and what does not.

By using good judgment, you will decide what no longer serves your character, what holds her back, and what needs to be cut.

In my work, I've seen people struggle with some common character traits: the shadow aspects of the rescuer, addict, student, mother, and gossip, all archetypes depicted in *The Fighter*. I chose these archetypes for this step, and I've also included the artist, since creative blockage is frustrating for many people, and I believe that creativity is essential for your health and well-being.

The Fighter, a true story, serves as the perfect example of what it means to do some difficult editing and to step into the light side of these archetypes—with amazing results.

Up to this point you have done a lot of storytelling. Your character has acknowledged her fears and realized that she is the writer of her life story. She's begun to listen to her director, embraced her archetypes, worked on becoming a better producer, taken center stage, learned her lines, found her supporting players, and set the stage by envisioning her desired future.

But here's the thing. Until she lets go of the things that no longer serve her, she'll never make any progress. I'm sure you've heard the saying,

"Nature abhors a vacuum." In this step, *Edit Your Film*, you are going to create that vacuum, or at least begin to clear the decks to make space for the good to come in. The role of the film editor is a crucial and a creative one, because the editor discerns not just the good from the bad, but the necessary scenes from the unnecessary ones, the characters who are dragging the protagonist down, and even the characters who no longer fit the story. Through expert editing, what's left is a great, cohesive movie.

If you don't edit the movie of your life, I can almost guarantee you that at some point, the universe will do it for you, and in a way that will rock your world. Not in the good, sweep-you-off-your-feet, romance-novel kind of way, but in the devastating, what-am-I-going-to-do-now kind of way. Life has a way of stepping in and removing things if, after a period of time of trying to get through to you, you don't heed its warnings. It's as though it finally throws its mighty fists up in the air in disgust and says, "Okay then, here you go. Good luck."

Like my friend who found out her husband was cheating on her, then her apartment caught fire and she lost most of her belongings. For years she ignored the voice that told her the marriage wasn't right and she truly wanted to live in New York. Holly was devastated, and it took a long time for her to bounce back. But she did. When life stepped in and forced her to make a change, she moved to New York, got a better job, met the man of her dreams, and had the family she always wanted. You can read Holly's story in my book *Stuck with Mr. Wrong? Ten Steps to Starring in Your Own Life Story*.

You cannot always prevent these events from happening. As you learned in step one, *Embrace Your Inner Screenwriter*, you don't have full control over the script you write, but you can be as proactive as possible and be an excellent editor of your life story.

In this step, you're going to contribute to your new life by removing the things, attitudes, and people that no longer resonate with who you are and what you want. You'll become skilled at recognizing when you need to do some editing. Exactly what needs to go will be clearer when you listen to your director. Out with the old will make room for the new.

First, let's do some inner work. The following archetypal characters, up until now, may have been boozing it up a little too much and doing some unhealthy, late-night partying with your inner film critic. We need to get them to step out of that shadow and give them new jobs, standing alongside your inner film director. The archetypes you studied in the first eight steps apply too, but let's check out a few new ones.

The Rescuer

You're a professional firefighter or EMT. Your sister's car broke down, and she needs you to pick her up. Your friend is going through a bad breakup. You're right there to lend your support, because you're a good person, operating on the light side of the rescuer archetype. Having a strong rescuer archetype in your psyche is a wonderful quality when applied in healthy ways.

But if your boyfriend is passed out drunk on the couch again, and you still think you can get him to stop drinking if you can just find the right strategy, you may be living in its shadow. If the good-looking catch on Match.com, whom you never met in real life, needs you to lend him a thousand dollars to help pay his son's medical expenses, and you do, then you may be living in its shadow. If a classmate you haven't seen in twenty years contacts you on Facebook and shares her relationship problems with you, and you think you're just the person to help her—not a parent, not a sibling, not a friend, but you, the person they haven't seen in decades—then you may be living in its shadow. If you think the person you've been dating will be perfect for you just as soon as you can help him heal the wounds from his abusive childhood and become...you know...available, then you may be living in its shadow. If you find yourself ranting and raving to friends about what they should (or shouldn't) do, and you lament the fact that they won't listen, then you may be living in its shadow.

Get the picture? You're a good person, so naturally you like to help, but editing requires that you distinguish healthy, empowered helping from codependency. Stop trying to rescue people who can only rescue themselves. Use good judgment. Surround yourself with people who will build you up—healthy, adult characters who know how to rescue themselves from their own mess. After all, they're the only ones who can. You can't do it for them.

Be like Glinda, the wise guide. Hand your friend the pamphlet to a twelve-step program, fade off into the distance in your cosmic bubble, and then let him make the journey. Don't kid yourself into being a fairy godmother. You don't have a magic wand or a white horse. And while we all come with a little baggage, especially as we get older, just make sure he's not looking to dump it on you. Tell him to find another pack mule. You're trying to get rid of stuff, not add more to the pile. Organizations such as Al-Anon, the sister group to Alcoholics Anonymous, are good resources if you think you are in a codependent relationship.

When it comes to the people you keep in your life, make the distinction between using good judgment and practicing non-judgment. This is something I learned the hard way when it came to the men I formed relationships with. If I had practiced good judgment, I would have listened to my intuition and realized that they were not going to be positive influences on my life. I confused using good judgment with being judgmental and made excuses for them. I've been in relationships with two alcoholics. Now I know that I can see a person's humanity and accept him, but still choose not to allow him in my inner circle, at least not on an intimate level.

When your antagonist is a person—a bad boss, toxic boyfriend, or questionable friend—you have choices in terms of your relationship.

1. End it. Completely edit them from your story. Leave your job or sever ties with that person.

2. Change it. Keep the person in your life but not in the same capacity. Maybe you have a great friendship, but the business partnership needs to go, for example.

3. Accept it. Stop trying to change this person and live with things the way they are.

Imagine the movie of your life and write the scene all three ways. Which one looks, sounds, and feels best for the story? What feelings come up for you?

Keep in mind what you learned in step three, *Become a Producer, Lead with Sovereignty*. Remember the connection between money, sex, and creativity. The demon of the second chakra is guilt, so maintaining an unhealthy relationship because you feel guilty ending it, even though you know it's causing you great harm, can be detrimental to your health. It's a no-win proposition.

The Addict

Do you suffer from any addictions? The shadow side of the addict won't just show up in the form of a dependency on alcohol, food, drugs, video games, or sex. It can manifest itself in other ways that seem inno-cent on the surface but are harmful to your life. Do you feel like you absolutely have to have something in your life in order to be happy?

I've come to view wrong relationships as cigarettes. You may try to "patch" things up and take breaks from them now and again. You may rationalize that there's enough good there to justify the habit, but you know they're bad for you. They'll never be good for you. No matter what you do, they'll always be a cigarette, and just like cigarettes, the only surefire way to break the addiction is to quit cold turkey before it does any long-term damage to your health and well-being.

If you're in a cigarette relationship, ask yourself what the long-term benefits are to sticking with it. If you determine there are none, or you find yourself rationalizing, you're in it out of habit. Go back and repeat steps one through eight. Notice if you have any issues with fear, guilt, shame, grief, lies (to yourself), or illusion, the demons of each chakra. Don't wait until you feel ready to take action, because you may never be. Quit cold turkey. Listen to the wisdom of your kind, emotionally intel-ligent inner director. Sit on your hands, delete their name and number from your cell phone, burn all their pictures, and jam-pack your sched-ule with other things to do until they finally leave your system and the urge to grab a butt eventually fades.

A close male friend of mine was the victim of a stalker. He was like a drug to her, and when he made it clear that he didn't want to have any-thing to do with her, he became her obsession. I've never seen anything like it. She went to great lengths to emotionally abuse and harass him, including phoning him incessantly, sending threatening e-mails and text messages, showing up at places where she knew he'd be, and standing outside his apartment building when he got home from work. She lied to the police and the court system to make it look like she was his victim in order to obtain a restraining order, which just emboldened her more. Her chief aim in life for a year was to try to force him to violate the order so that he'd be arrested. She even crafted fake e-mails and submitted them to the police to try to make it look as though he was contacting her through a third party. He, along with two others in his close circle, eventually succeeded in obtaining harassment orders against her, but in order to free himself from the abusive grips of her addiction, he had to move across the country. Obviously, she crossed a line from addiction into some sort of mental illness, but I'm sure you get where I'm coming from.

Are you overly committed to the outcome of things? Are you so fixated on your vision that you wouldn't be able to notice an even better resolution to your story than you have imagined? If so, you may have made the predetermination that your way is the only right way. In other words, you're addicted to it. Have a vision, but be open to other options.

The light side of the addict is there to show you when you are becoming dependent on someone or something so that you may take steps to break that pattern of behavior. Look to your supporting players; groups, therapists, or other professionals can help you if you suffer from an addiction. Commit to get rid of it. It's blocking your progress.

The next step, *Accept Your Oscar*, is about the concept of nonattachment and the seventh, or crown, chakra. This chakra also relates to editing your film, since attachment is the demon of this chakra, and addictions are obviously unhealthy attachments.

The Student

The student archetype is an interesting one. I love learning. It goes hand in hand with teaching, but the shadow student won't allow you to acknowledge that you know enough. If you've ever felt as if you weren't smart enough, educated enough, or experienced enough—even though you know you are, truly—your shadow student needs to put on her cap and gown and graduate already, then step into the light where your inner film director hangs out. Your director appreciates that your character is open to learning new things and can approach everything with just enough of a beginner's mind to succeed. But notice if you are clinging to continued education as a way to avoid having to take responsibility for your career, business, hobby, or whatever it is that you've been absorbed in. You don't need to take every course out there and have every certification and degree before you start. There are many ways to learn, including through books, videos, and mentorships. Tune into the words of your inner director and decide if you need to edit doubt about the extent of your knowledge. If you legitimately need more training, get it, but if you don't, you know enough. *You just need to believe it.*

Dorothy became the enlightened student when she finally stopped looking to an authority figure for answers. When she discovered that the Wizard was just a man, and Glinda told her she had the power to return home all along—she just had to figure it out for herself—Dorothy stepped out of the shadow student role and became her own authority figure. Micky Ward was kept in a student role by his mother, whose main focus was on her eldest son, the "experienced" fighter. He finally steps into the light when he stands up to his mother in a scene you can view in your Star Pack.

The Mother

The word *mother* conjures up images of someone who nurtures and provides unconditional love. The shadow side of this archetype is the mother who goes too far—the smothering mother, today known as the helicopter parent. She doesn't want her child to develop independence. Alice Ward is an example of a loving but controlling mother. She controls Micky with guilt and manipulation, which is difficult for anyone to break free from. But in the end, she stands by his side.

The Artist

I believe that we are all artists in some way. We are, by nature, creative. You may be artistic in the traditional sense. Maybe you write, play music, paint, act, or dance. If you derive great pleasure from the way you take care of your home, garden, or some sort of hobby, you are an artist. Being creative is essential to your well-being, but many live on the shadow side of this archetype, the "starving artist." If you believe that engaging in anything that isn't work-related or money-making is pointless, or if you stop yourself from doing something creative because you know you will never be a professional or even produce something of monetary value, then you are listening to your inner critic. You need to listen to your director, because that desire to create is there for a reason. It may be there to help you ease an addiction, find more joy in your everyday life, or take your focus off a particular challenge. Engaging in something creative, even if it has nothing to do with your job, often results in new ideas and insights in other areas of your life. I can look back on my career and see how several promotions I received came on the heels of a creative endeavor outside of work. As you learned from step three, *Become a Producer*, and your second chakra, creative expression is essential to your health. Without some sort of creative pursuit, you may look to money and sex or something else to fulfill you, which never works, at least not long-term. Unfortunately, some people view art for art's sake, or creating something for the simple enjoyment of it, as a waste of time. This is narrow-minded and shortsighted, and unfortunately, common in our culture. Music and art are the first classes to be cut in our schools when budgets are tight.

The Gossip

What's left to talk about if you can't talk about other people? Okay, just kidding. Starring in your own life story is about stepping fully into your power and scripting your life in a way that honors faith over fear, and with trust that you are on a wonderful path toward your highest and best self. Why waste time on other people's issues? It's a terrible feeling to find out someone has spread rumors about you or betrayed your confidence. The inner gossip will appear as a reminder to respect another person's boundaries, stay silent, and hold their story in confidence. Bringing other people up in conversation isn't gossip, but betraying them is. Gossiping can result throat chakra issues.

I wasn't surprised when a former colleague was diagnosed with a hyperactive thyroid. She didn't hesitate to talk about people behind their backs, and not in a good way. She had a hard time containing her jealousy. Other thyroid or throat issues could be attributed to the opposite problem—not saying how you feel and keeping it bottled up inside instead. I'm not saying that every throat or thyroid disorder is a result of gossip or passivity, but if you see yourself in either light, and you happen to have issues in this chakra, you may want to consider giving up this pastime. Go back to step six, *Learn Your Lines*, and practice assertiveness. Your audience will thank you. Micky Ward's sisters were terrible gossips and pretty hilarious with their big "nasty" hair (as Charlene called it). Without getting to know Charlene, they already prejudged her and referred to her as an "MTV

Girl." You can view a scene in your Star Pack where they completely lost control of themselves and got into a fight on her front porch.

Willie Wonka was a powerful editor, wasn't he? While the children may have done it to themselves, the whole purpose of his contest was to find the right child to inherit his factory. Like a reality-show contestant, each child was taken out one by one; Augustus the glutton, Violet the gum addict, Veruca the entitled brat, and Mike the TV addict. He didn't feel bad about the children when they fell into the chocolate river, blew up like a blueberry, fell down the garbage chute, or wound up three inches tall. They had some life lessons to learn, and he didn't stand in their way. Neither should you when it comes to people whose behavior has a negative impact on your life. Charlie, the boy best suited to take over the chocolate factory, was the only contestant left standing in the end. Winners know when and where to cut.

The same is true for Dorothy. The Wizard was really an aspect of her. She knew on a subconscious level that she had to cut Gulch from her story, i.e., "kill the witch"—in other words, face her fears. Only in a dream can it be done that way, but in real life, she would have had to stand up to her in some fashion. The script in the opening of this chapter is a metaphor for what you need to do in order to have your "requests" granted. You need to eliminate the things standing in your way. I'm not sure why it feels so dangerous to do so. ("But what if she kills us first?" said the lion.) But as we learned from Dorothy, it's often scarier in our head than it is in reality.

External Editing

Clutter creates stuck energy. It's like driving down the highway during rush hour stuck in bumper-to-bumper traffic. Progress is slow and frustrating. Compare this to clearing your space and going on a road trip—top down in your sports car, sixty-five miles per hour on the perfect sunny day, hair blowing in the breeze—a true Grace Kelly moment.

I will admit that I am completely fascinated by the *Hoarders* reality programs. In case you're not quite clear on how important this step is, watch the show. While hoarding is an extreme example of an inability to let go of what no longer serves you, I think it is as a powerful illustration for the importance of this step.

Whenever I happen to catch *Hoarders, Buried Alive*, I wind up glued to the TV set. Like watching a train wreck, I can't help myself. It amazes me how people live like that—piles upon piles of junk fill their homes from floor to ceiling until there's barely a path to walk through. There was one episode where a man held onto so much crap that he wound up living on the streets. The only way he could enter his New York City apartment was through the fire escape. When people came to help him sort through and discard his things, he grew agitated and angry.

There have been episodes where the cleaning crew found the remains of the family cat lost among a pile of garbage (inside the home). The cat had gone missing at some point, but no one knew where he'd gone. After a while, they must have assumed he ran away. Suffice it to say their olfactory senses must have been deadened over time. The therapists who help these people clearly have hearts of gold and ironclad stomachs.

One woman couldn't stop collecting ventriloquist dummies. Another poor man hoarded thousands of rats. Rats! There were so many of them, you couldn't see the floor. Watching him spread grain across the living room carpet reminded me of farms and chicken coops. Somewhere a wire got crossed, that's for sure. But the man was sweet. He insisted that the mothers and their babies be captured together. He didn't want to break up any families during the eviction process.

The common denominator among people who hoard is emotional trauma. Something in their lives triggers an irrational need to hold onto every object. They attach sentimental value to the most banal of things, like empty tuna fish cans. It's clearly a mental illness, and it has a sad effect on not only the hoarder but on his or her family, who must deal with the filth and embarrassment created by this person they love. The accumulation of junk creates a toxic environment. It isn't uncommon for the cleaning crew to find evidence of mice, insects, E. coli bacteria, and mold. In some cases the house is on the verge of being condemned. Allowing things to pile up and rot causes structural damage to the house itself, just as holding onto things, people, jobs, and other things that no longer serve you can cause damage to your life and even your body.

If clutter is noise, then no wonder it's so difficult for friends and family to get through to hoarders. Hoarding is an addiction. They can't be rescued. Like trying to convince an addict to give up drinking, you can't persuade them to throw things away. Their situations are heartbreaking. It isn't what they want, yet these poor people are absolutely gripped by fear over what will happen to them if they let go of what to you and me are useless objects. On these programs, the hoarder takes the first step to recovery from any addiction, which is acknowledging that there's a problem. The therapist then guides them in taking the next step, usually in the direction of a gigantic Dumpster.

Hoarders provide an extreme example of how necessary it is to edit unnecessary things from your life story. If having that much stuff can destroy your relationships, health, and life in general, imagine what a pile of paper that you keep meaning to sort through, a dresser full of clothes you never wear, or any other mess you keep avoiding, is doing to your psyche little by little. Editing unnecessary objects from your life will give you a boost in energy.

That takes care of some physical stuff. How about people? Is there anyone in your life that you need to say good-bye to, such as an argumentative, provocative Facebook "friend" or cigarette relationship? Perhaps even more difficult than things are the people who no longer serve your story, which is why I chose *The Fighter* for this step. This award-winning film serves as the perfect example of what it means to do some difficult editing in your life. If you have a tough time saying no to people or establishing healthy boundaries, then definitely take the time to see the movie. One of the hardest things to do is edit people from your life. This doesn't always mean ending a relationship, but it can mean changing the nature of the relationship.

What I loved about *The Fighter* is that not only is it a perfect example for this step, but it showed how all of the characters moved out of the shadow aspects of their characters. Dicky Ecklund conquers his addiction after serving time in prison and eventually comes back as one of Micky's trainers. Alice loosens her control over Micky to support him and stops denying her son's addiction. Micky "graduates" from being Dicky's underling and steps fully into the ring as a professional. It's implied that they all embraced Charlene in the end instead of gossiping behind her back as well.

Micky's Transformation

ACT 2

Mind
Develop winner's mindset

Heart
Love himself enough to
honor his dreams

Courage
Edit family as business
partners

ACT 1

ACT 3

Challenge:
Addicted brother and
controlling mother.

Resolution:
Wins big fight.
Family celebrates
with him

Summary

To star in your own life story, you need use good judgment, decide what doesn't belong in your life, and make a conscious choice to edit all of it from your script. Practice non-judgment, but don't be afraid to remove things that don't serve your story to make room for the good to come in. Examine your relationship to the rescuer, addict, artist, student, mother, and gossip archetypes, as well as any other archetypes you resonate with most.

Determine where you need to step out of the shadows to embrace their lighter aspects. Clear space in your physical environment, because editing your surroundings, as well as your beliefs and attitudes, will help you to create space for your vision to manifest. You are not obligated to keep a relationship just because it exists. Cut out any unnecessary characters, whether it's through ending a relationship completely, changing it, or accepting it as it is. Look at everything—your nutrition, exercise habits, self-care, image, and clothing. Notice what you listen to and watch and the impact it has on your mood and energy level. Don't ignore these things, because they aren't trivial. They matter. Take a stand for yourself and what you want in your life.

Editing is the art of creating by removal. In the on-line course we do a guided visualization that will put you in the audience's seat of your life, assessing what to let go of to create the life you desire to become your best self. This exercise will help you to identify areas where you are afraid of letting go—of what could happen if you "destroy the witch" as Dorothy was instructed to do in the opening scene of this chapter.

Notes

Notes

STEP TEN

Accept Your Oscar

Lead with Nonattachment

The Color Purple

SHUG
More than anything God love admiration.

CELIE
You saying God is vain?

SHUG

No, not vain, just wanting to share a good
thing. I think it pisses God off when you walk
by the colour purple in a field
and don't notice it.

CELIE
You saying it just wanna be loved
like it say in the Bible?

SHUG
Yeah, Celie. Everything wanna be loved. Us
sing and dance, and holla just wanting to
be loved. Look at them trees. Notice how
the trees do everything people do to get
attention... except walk? [they laugh]
Oh Miss Celie, I feels like singing!

The Color Purple

O n the opening scene of The Color Purple, two young girls, Celie (Whoopi Goldberg) and her sister Nettie (Akoshua Busia), are playing in a field. Celie is about to give birth to her second child by an abusive stepfather, Alphonso. He takes both of her children away as soon as they're born. It's rumored that they are adopted by a minister and his wife.

Albert Johnson (Danny Glover), a widower with three children, asks Alphonso if he can marry Nettie. Alphonso refuses, but offers Celie. Albert accepts his offer, even though Celie is considered the uglier of the two girls. She refers to Albert as "Mister" and goes to live with him as his wife, maid, childcare provider, and whipping post. Celie goes from one abusive home to another. She is completely submissive.

When Alphonso starts coming on to Nettie, she runs away to live with Celie. She attends school and then comes home to teach Celie how to read. There is a sense of urgency to her lessons since Mister is starting to make passes at Nettie, and the two girls know it's only a matter of time before he gets physical. Sure enough, on her way to school one day, Mister tries to attack her. She hits him with her book bag and kicks him in the groin. She runs home to Celie, but he forces her to leave. Nettie promises to write, but Mister vows that she will never see or hear from her again and forbids Celie from ever touching the mailbox. Celie never receives any letters and assumes she is dead.

In the second act, she meets Shug Avery, a lounge singer with a bad reputation and Albert's off-and-on mistress. They become friends after Shug gets sick and Celie nurses her back to health. The two women also become lovers for a short period of time.

Mister's children grow up, and Harpo marries Miss Sofia (Oprah Winfrey). They marry for love, but their relationship is wrought with trouble when Mister (and Celie, interestingly) advises Harpo to beat Miss Sofia, but unlike Celie, Sofia isn't one to stand back and take it. She fights back, and in between the fights, they have three children. Sofia eventually can't take any more and leaves Harpo. Harpo finds a new girlfriend named Squeak and turns their home into a juke joint.

In town one day, the mayor's wife, Miss Millie, asks Sofia to work as her maid. Sofia replies with an indignant, "Hell no!"

The mayor slaps her across the face. She returns the blow, knocking the mayor down, for which she is sent to jail for eight years. She is eventually released, but her spirit is crushed. Sofia winds up working as Miss Millie's maid after all.

Years pass and Shug eventually marries. She and her new husband come by for a visit, and on a trip to the mailbox, she finds a letter addressed to Celie from Nettie. Celie was unaware of the fact that her sister had been writing to her for years. While the men get drunk and leave for Harpo's juke joint, they search for the missing letters and find a stack hidden underneath a floor board in Albert's closet. Celie discovers that her two biological children were, in fact, adopted by a minister and his wife, and her sister Nettie was also taken in by the family. They moved to Africa as missionaries. Her letters take days for Celie to read. She sneaks them between pages of her Bible and church hymnal, and she finds her confidence growing with every word. Through her friendship with Shug, who has essentially become her primary supporting player, Celie slowly connects with her personal power, gains self-confidence, and overcomes her fears of what will happen to her if she stands up to her jackass of a husband and leaves him. Her frustration and anger culminate in a powerful scene where she tells him off at the dinner table. Her newfound confidence inspires Sofia as well.

Celie leaves with Shug and her husband. On her way out, Mister tries everything to beat her down and tear at her self-esteem. But she is no longer the same, submissive person that she once was.

She tells Mister, "Until you do right by me, everything you do is going to fail."

In one of the most moving pieces of the film, Shug starts to sing at the juke joint but is interrupted by the choir at her estranged father's church singing *Maybe God is Tryin' to Tell You Somethin'* (Star Pack). Shug's father, the minister, hasn't spoken to her for years. Her own children were being raised by her parents. When Shug hears the choir, she stops and starts to sing along, then leads everyone from the bar over to the church. She comes through the back door to face her father. He steps down from the pulpit, and the two embrace.

Albert goes to his mailbox and finds another letter addressed to Celie from the immigration service. Mister finds it in his heart to send money to Nettie so that she can come back to America.

Alphonso dies, and Celie inherits the home which, it turns out, was owned by a biological father she never knew, and willed to Celie and her sister. Celie opens up a shop sewing pants downtown.

In the final scene, a car drives down the road out past the field in front of Celie's house where Shug, Harpo, Sofia, and other family members are visiting. She thinks the people have lost their way, until they step out of the car, and their bright red and purple scarves wave like flags in the passing breeze. Celie realizes who it is and runs to her sister. They are finally reunited after thirty years, and Celie meets her children, Adam and Olivia.

Nonattachment

"The Law of Detachment says that in order to acquire anything in the physical universe, you have to relinquish your attachment to it."

From the *Seven Spiritual Laws of Success* by Deepak Chopra

"Detachment implies a sense of withdrawal... Nonattachment simply implies not holding on."

Joseph Goldstein

http://meaningoflife.tv/transcript.php?speaker=goldstein

Accept your Oscar
Lead with Nonattachment

Nine years ago, I was looking for a new home. I took out a piece of paper and made a list of everything I wanted in a house. I wanted at least two bathrooms and three bedrooms. There needed to be plenty of space for the boys to play. I didn't want something that needed any repairs—a newer home was preferable. I wasn't looking for a mansion, but I was determined to find something beautiful within my price range. At the time, my needs were simple and practical. I wanted a warm, comfortable home in which to raise my two sons, and I wanted to live in the downtown area of a community with a good school system. After I had it all down on paper, I filed it away for safekeeping.

I began by searching Realtor.com for houses in the towns I thought would work for us. While it was fun in some respects—I loved going to open houses and getting to know the ins and outs of finding a place to live, I was frustrated, too. Most of the single family homes in my price range needed a lot of work.

We needed to stay in Massachusetts, but I had trouble figuring out where. I grew up on the South Shore and lived there for twelve years with my ex-husband, but going back didn't feel right. At the same time, living on the North Shore was difficult. My children's father still lived on the South Shore, and driving back and forth to see him took hours. I loved the town we were living in—Hamilton. We'd made many friends there and if things had worked out differently, we probably would have stayed. But it wasn't practical.

I described in step eight how I prayed for guidance and listened to my dreams for clues. In a dream I came to a fork in the road. A sign appeared that said, "Wrentham" and an arrow pointed left. I casually looked on-line to see what was for sale in Wrentham, but the only thing available that met most of my criteria was a townhouse condominium, and I didn't want to live in a condo. I decided that maybe I was being guided to look in the general area, so I started searching nearby towns and considered purchasing a blue ranch in Sharon. It met most of my criteria—number of bedrooms, bathrooms, etc., but something didn't feel right about it, so I didn't buy it.

After several more months of searching, I finally took a break. Life got busy and I was getting discouraged. But then my sense of urgency arose again. Rather than despair and indulge that it's-never-going-to-happen voice, I slowed down and turned inward for guidance. I had a second dream where I was standing outside the home I'd almost purchased in Sharon, only the house in my dream was beige, not blue like it was in real life. There were construction workers on the roof, as though they were repairing it or putting on a second story. In the dream I wanted to know if the house was still for sale. I looked left and saw a For Sale sign with a bright red cardinal on it with woods in the background. Written on it was Forest Park Realty. When I woke up, I said to myself, *if the name of the condo association has anything to do with woods or forest.*

I immediately logged onto my computer to see if the condo in Wrentham was still for sale. It was beige, like the home in my dream. It also had a second floor, unlike the blue ranch in Sharon. When I looked on Realtor.com, I found that it was still for sale, and the condo association's name was Forest Park Condo Association. I was floored. How could I *not* look? I finally listened, called the realtor, and took the drive south that cold day in February to see about a townhouse. The whole way down, there was a part of me that thought it was silly. I was checking out a house in a town I'd only been to once before, based on a dream.

"That's what crazy people do," said my inner film critic, Pia.

"Don't all wonderful things in life start with a dream?" said my inner film director.

"Well, just don't tell anybody. They'll think you're a little out there," Pia cautioned.

I knew as soon as I walked in the front door that this was our home. The woman who owned it kept it immaculate. It had been built only four years before, so everything still felt new. I had a gut feeling that I would "know" my house, and that I would recognize when it was the right time to buy based on that feeling. This was the first time I'd felt it. While other houses I'd viewed may have met some or most of my criteria, this house was different. I experienced that sense of knowing—like knowing he or she is "the one." Two months later, we were living in our new home in Wrentham.

This step, *Accept Your Oscar, Lead with Nonattachment,* is about celebrating how far you've come and acknowledging all you've done, but it's also about releasing your need to have everything turn out exactly as you envisioned and in the timeframe you think it should happen. It's about releasing your attachment to it, whatever *it* is. Easier said than done, right?

After we moved into this house, I was going through some papers and found the list I'd created the year before. When I wrote it, I expected to find a home much more quickly than I did. And I'd love to be able to tell you that I was completely at peace the entire time I waited, but I wasn't. I had many moments where I was discouraged and even felt panicky. It wasn't just about me. This was about my ability to provide for my boys. What helped me keep my chin up was the ability to tune in to my inner director. I knew discouragement was a sign I wasn't listening to my intuition. I was being impatient. Allowing negativity to get me down wouldn't help anything. I did my part in searching, but I remained open to what would happen. I did my best to make peace with life in the meantime.

Finding our house happened at the right time, just not in my impatient, I-want-it-now time. When I look back, I see that it happened when I was really ready. It took me some time to finally let go of the relationship, even though deep down I knew it wasn't working. I'd also grown to love Hamilton, the friends we'd made, and our lifestyle. I lived across the street from a yoga studio, and within walking distance of the boys' school, my train to work, a couple of great restaurants, and two yarn shops. We were also within fifteen minutes of the ocean, which I miss now more than anything. Those things were hard to give up, but I finally reached the moment when I was ready to leave.

What amazed me as I looked at the list again a year later, is how close to finding everything we came, but what astounded me even more is that we got even better than what I had asked for.

The price of the townhouse came down sixty thousand dollars from its original listing price, so had I found it any sooner, it would have cost more than I could have afforded. We didn't find a house with two bathrooms. This one had three. It didn't just have three standard bedrooms. The third bedroom was the size of our two-car garage and had a walk-in closet with its own private bath. I thought I wanted a single family home, but living in a three-unit townhouse has actually given us more privacy and relief from the responsibilities of lawn care and snow removal. For a single mother, these services have turned out to be a godsend. I didn't think I wanted a condo, but being in an association with only two other families has worked out well.

There was something on my list that we didn't get. The house wasn't located in a downtown area. I decided that was more of a nice-to-have than a need-to-have, so it wasn't a deal breaker, but what's interesting is that the house abutted state forest, something that never occurred to me to wish for. We moved into a home with acres upon acres of conservation land, right out our back door. This was perfect for the boys. One of the things I felt bad about leaving in Hamilton was Patton Pond, because my younger son, Christopher, loved to go there to catch frogs. It's here in this townhouse in Wrentham, located close to the highway but tucked back against the woods, that I began writing. One of my first stories was called *The Art of Catching a Bullfrog*, published in *Aspire* magazine (Star Pack), about Christopher's love for catching bullfrogs in the vernal pool out back. We not only found what I wanted, but also what we needed. I couldn't have scripted this entire thing myself—I couldn't have scripted it *better* myself. It wasn't in my consciousness. By remaining unattached to the exact thing that I thought we wanted, and because I remained open to divine timing, I was able to receive exactly what was right for us.

Our house in Wrentham was my Academy Award for stepping into my starring role as the leading lady in my life story. For the first time in years, my home is full of peace, creativity, laughter, and love—the exact environment I wanted for us.

The Seventh Chakra: Crown

The seventh chakra is located at the crown of the head. It pertains to your muscular system, skeletal system, and skin. It is in this chakra that you develop trust and an ability to see the big picture of your life. In the crown chakra you connect with your spirituality, find inspiration, keep the faith, and remain open to the divine. The demon of the seventh chakra is *attachment*. Its element is thought, and its color is white or purple.

We've all experienced moments where we have ideas—start a business, change careers, write a screenplay, join a band, scale back, etc. An idea comes down through your crown chakra. From there, it works its way to your third-eye chakra, where you begin to use your imagination and intuition to form a clear vision of this inspiration. The next stop is the throat, or your source of will, where you'll either deny its existence or give voice to it. From there it goes to your heart chakra, where you'll get in touch with how you feel about it. Do you love this idea? Does it feel right? Are your head and heart in alignment? Next comes your solar plexus—your gut. Do you have the self-confidence to bring this idea to fruition? Then to your sacral chakra, where you'll ask yourself questions about the financial reality of the idea, what kind of impact it may have your intimate relationships, and the creative satisfaction that may come from it, and then down to your root chakra source of survival, where you'll address your fears.

At any point, you may kill the idea. It may seem too risky. Maybe your heart's not in it or you won't have the willpower to follow through. Sometimes, that's okay. But as you've learned through this book, when you know, deep down, it's something you're meant to do, it will continue to nag you until you do something about it. The energetic connection between your chakras and your physical body is a strong one, and your inability to move ahead with it may cause you to feel out of alignment, feel pain or discomfort in certain areas of your body, or even become ill. In this book, you began by looking at the root chakra, because this is where you take the first step in addressing anything that's blocking your idea from coming to fruition. The idea may come from the top down, but you identify what's stopping you by going from the bottom up—like a grassroots movement in your life, although it isn't necessarily such a linear process.

Say you have an idea one day, seemingly out of the blue, that you want to do body work for a living. You no longer want to work in a corporate environment. You want something completely different. Your current career may have been exciting at one point, but it has lost its luster. It no longer brings you the same sense of satisfaction. You may not understand it, because you've established a life around your corporate career. You're making a great living, and you've grown accustomed to a certain lifestyle. This new idea could be incredibly strong, but it feels like a disruption in your life.

But you'll begin to see yourself in a spa, you can smell essential oils, hear the sound of calming music, and feel the ambience of a candlelit room. The more you see it, the more you will want to talk about it. You may run the idea by your husband or a friend and share how this is something you've always wanted to do. He'll look at you from across the dinner table and smile. He'll tell you to go for it. From there, you may begin to love the thought of it. As you sit in another business meeting, looking at Gant charts and financial projections, your heart will ache. It doesn't feel right. This isn't where you belong.

You'll look at your finances and figure out how you can make it work, knowing it may take a few years to fill your practice. Then you'll look into schools and enroll in evening classes. The first night, you'll remember how, as a young child, you were excited for the first day of school. You're bursting-at-the-seams excited by all the things you're learning and about the prospect of shifting from your career to your vocation.

You know you've been called to do this work. You're afraid, but you're doing it anyway. You have faith that this idea has been divinely given to you, and it's your job to fulfill it.

Review that paragraph and substitute your dream or desire for the example, becoming a body worker. Go down the chakras and notice where your idea is sabotaged or aborted. Perhaps you don't have a supportive spouse. You may need to figure out what his or her fears may be. Maybe your financial circumstances aren't in good enough shape to support this idea yet—it isn't the right time, or you need to do more prep work (make a budget, take a second job, simplify your life to save money).

Someone with a healthy, balanced crown chakra isn't attached to the outcome of things. They are able to let go, trust, and surrender. Even though throughout this process you have been developing a vision for your life, in this step—and in the crown chakra—you also release the need to be right and to think there's only one way of doing, being, or having something. When you ask for assistance from a higher power through prayer or meditation, you are connecting with that source through your crown chakra.

> "When I thought I couldn't go on, I forced myself to keep going. My success is based on persistence, not luck."
>
> —Estee Lauder

Someone with a healthy crown chakra sees the divine in everyone. You are a divine being. Knowing this, will you treat yourself any differently? Will you go easier on yourself? Will you take the time to honor and respect your achievements? Will you plan for the future, live in the present, and remain open to whatever surprises life may have in store for you?

Someone with an imbalance in their crown chakra may live on the shadow side of the addict archetype. They may be overly fixated on a particular belief system, spiritual practice, or absolute insistence that there is only one right way of being or believing in this world. They are closed off to spiritual guidance, because they've basically chosen to live in a box of set beliefs. Nothing else is allowed in, so accessing their intuition is extremely difficult. If your intuition tells you something that goes against your beliefs, it's extremely hard to heed its guidance.

The demon of this chakra is attachment. To open the seventh chakra requires that you stay open to possibility, ask questions, examine your thoughts and beliefs, and consider something new. You are willing to receive inspiration in whatever package it comes in, and to trust that it will come at the right time and in the right way—which may not be *your* time or *your* way. To be balanced and healthy in the crown chakra is to practice patience and to get in touch with your intuition, which knows when something feels right.

Veruca Salt's favorite line in *Willie Wonka and the Chocolate Factory* is "I want it now," and her father is quick to try to give her whatever she wants. She's a brat. When my children were little, whenever we went to a department store, they would invariably see something they wanted and start asking me for it. If they were particularly obnoxious about it, I would play the role of Veruca Salt and recite my favorite lines, complete with the fake British accent.

"I want the goose that lays the golden eggs! I want an Oompa Loompa! I want it *now*, Daddy!"

This had the effect of making them laugh while embarrassing them at the same time—a very effective parenting technique that I highly recommend for those of you with children who think nothing of having you spend endless amounts of money on impulse items.

We adults suffer from the same problem; we just do it in our heads. In our minds, we are constantly playing the role of Veruca Salt. We are incredibly hard on ourselves. I want this book to be finished now. When I first started writing it, I wanted it done in a few weeks, not months. So many people go into business for themselves thinking it will take off immediately, and when it doesn't, they feel like failures and close shop before giving it a chance. As a manager, I had people report to me who were dissatisfied if they weren't promoted within a year. When you're looking for your life partner, you want to find him or her now. I hate being patient. I want it now, too, but that's not how life works.

The Wizard of Oz would have been an incredibly short film if Glinda had waved that magic wand over Dorothy's head and she instantly appeared in the Emerald City. She had to walk the long, yellow brick road and figure it out for herself. And so do you. We all do. Read any celebrity biography and most will tell you that their overnight success actually took years. The exceptions may be child actors, but considering the way many of them turn out, clearly easy success isn't always such a good thing. Albert Einstein worked in a patent office. Bill Gates started in his garage. Wayne Dyer sold books out of the back of his Ford Pinto before he became well known. Inventors go through trial and error, often for years, before discovering what works. Start-up companies often operate at a loss before becoming profitable. Many entrepreneurs try out different business ventures before finding one that succeeds. Weight loss is a daily choice to eat a little bit less and exercise a little bit more. Starting your own business requires beginning with a part-time venture on the side. You have to kiss a lot of frogs. Most everything takes time. Yet we've been fed a line that I think has created a lot of suffering: "You don't have to work hard. You have to work smart."

What is that? It's a lie, or at least the first part of that statement is a lie. You *do* have to work hard. It's hard to lose weight. It's hard to start your own business. It's hard to leave a relationship. It's hard to commit. It's hard to change jobs. It's hard to learn something new. It's hard to write a book. It's hard to go back to school. Few people get to where they want to be without hard work. The key is to work hard at something that you enjoy—or at least enjoy it *enough*, because most things come with some element you won't especially like.

What does being smart have to do with it? I realize that expression comes from the mindset that you can work hard and make little, and you can work smart and become a millionaire. I get it. It's smart to devote your energies to what you're good at, and to delegate when you can, but you can't skip the working hard part. Even smart people work hard—they just work hard at things they like. Something as seemingly awful as losing weight can be fun if it means taking a cooking light class or an exercise class that makes you feel good, instead of choosing a punishing workout that someone else swears by but you loathe.

Do any of these statements ring true for you?

"I want to lose 20 pounds, but I want to be thinner now. I can't wait three months."

"I want a master's degree, but I don't want it to take two years. Just the thought of it makes me want to go lie down."

"I want to write a book, but I don't want to have to get up every morning to write it. I just want it to flow right out of me."

"I love painting, but I don't have time."

"I'm in pain over a recent breakup, but I don't want to wait for time to heal me, I want to feel better now."

"I want a golden ticket! I want a goose that lays the golden eggs! I want an Oompa Loompa! I want it now, Daddy!"

This is where you can get stuck. In your desire to have it all resolve now, you do nothing and achieve no effect at all. You stay stuck in your story's first act, waiting and hoping for something or someone to change—to rescue you from your plight. You can stay stuck here for years, if not a lifetime. Even if you do eventually achieve your desires, it comes at a cost: your precious present—what's in your life now.

Impatience can cause you to focus on the problem instead of the solution. The law of attraction states, "That which is like unto itself is drawn," so when you only have that initial glimpse at your dream, without the emotion of belief to back it up, you get stuck in the frustration of your present state, the I-want-it-but-I-can't-do-what's-required-to-get-it mindset, and there you stay. You may feign attempts to resolve the problem. You may dabble in your dreams now and again, but never fully commit. You may pull the guitar out of the closet, play a few chords, and then put it back as soon as your fingers get sore or you come across a chord you don't know yet. You may invest hundreds of dollars on diet pills that promise easy weight loss, or buy the next as-seen-on-TV gadget or get-rich-quick scheme. The eight-week training program collects dust on the shelf. You can spend your life replaying a fantasy career in your mind and wake up every morning to "I've Got You Babe," only to realize you're not getting anywhere. Or you can decide to take the first step and learn how to enjoy your life in the meantime.

Had I stopped looking for a house—or settled for one I didn't really want because I was too impatient to wait—who knows where we would have ended up? Perhaps this is how people wind up married to the wrong person—they are ready now, so it means whoever they meet in the now must be the one. They marry because they are at that age or place in life, rather than at that age and place and with that right person. They settle for the first job they are offered, because they're afraid if they don't take it, nothing better will come along and they will have missed an opportunity for at least a job. They listen to the voice of fear that tells them to make poor choices or give in to societal clichés and generalizations.

For a good laugh, watch the movie *What's Your Number*. Ally Darling (Anna Farris) buys into a Marie Claire article that tells her she's had twice as many lovers as the national average and therefore, she has a slim chance of ever getting married. She's already at twenty, so she spends the entire film trying to find each of her former lovers to see if any of them have become husband material, just so that she doesn't go over the number twenty. Her neighbor, a commitment-phobic Don Juan named Colin Shea (Chris Evans), helps her find each of the men. He thinks it's all completely ridiculous and tells her, "Who cares how many men you've slept with?" but because of that article, the story that's stuck in her head is "I'm never going to get married if I go over the number twenty."

She comes close to committing to an old boyfriend because she's now convinced he'd be perfect, plus the fact that her mother and friends approve of him. It takes a while for her to accept the fact that she loves Colin. Her transformation means letting go of the belief and story about the number twenty, and accepting who she is, a "jobless whore who's slept with twenty guys" (her words). The movie's hilarious, but

> *"Life is what happens to you when you're busy making other plans."*
>
> —*John Lennon*

it's also so true. We buy into clichés, stereotypes, social generalizations, tradition, other people's ideas of what is right for us, and all sorts of things, instead of buying into our own inner wisdom. Impatience and disempowering stories can kill dreams.

How to Manage Living in the Meantime

The Free Online Dictionary by Farlex defines the word "meantime" as the time between one occurrence and another; an interval.

If you break the word down it begins with the word "mean" and ends with the word "time." "Mean" is defined as average or middle, but it can feel like life being cruel or unkind. When you really want something badly, the meantime can feel like you're the guest of honor at a pity party hosted by your inner film critic. How many times have you felt as though you were being punished for something because life wasn't giving you what you wanted?

But "mean" can also be defined as a verb. It means "to act as a symbol of; signify or represent; to design, intend, or destine for a certain purpose or end." Looked at this way, the "meantime" can be viewed as the time where you set your intentions and make your plans. You can choose to believe that this time is just as important as the time when you reach your desired goal. Happiness research has found that the significant events in life, such as new romantic relationships, promotions, and awards, don't necessarily make us any happier over a long period of time than the little things in life. (Harvard Business Review—January-February 2012). Considered this way, it's crazy to view the meantime as a time of pain and suffering on your way to achieving your goals. Better to spend it with friends. Read a great book. Take long walks. Go on vacation. Learn something new. Engage in a hobby you thoroughly enjoy, or do something for someone else that will make them happy, which in turns makes you feel good.

Notice how viewing the meantime as an adjective places you in the victim role, whereas viewing it as a verb places you in the role of the hero. What if the meantime turns out to be one of your best times?

As I write this, I am in a meantime in many ways. I'm between boyfriends, and I would like to be in a loving, committed, relationship. I'd like to meet the love of my life and grow old with him. I could give in to fears that I'm too old, there are no good guys left, it'll never happen for me, and all that. Believe me, I have these fears, but when I indulge them, it doesn't do me any good. If anything, it creates a "meantime" that's full of suffering and causes me to make poor dating choices. Instead, I shift my focus to the things that bring me joy—yoga, my children, friends, writing, knitting, going on dates, and giving thought to what I truly desire in a partner.

I'm experiencing an in-between stage in my career. I'm having the same fears and anxieties I had with my last book when I was almost done writing it. I'm having all those what-if thoughts...*what if nobody likes it...what if it sucks...what if nobody buys it...what if I'm not supposed to be a writer or speaker...what if I go broke?* The list goes on. But then I remind myself that being a writer doesn't mean that writing is the only thing in my life. It's a part of it, but it isn't my sole purpose. Sometimes I enjoy the process of writing, but sometimes I don't. In fact it can be quite painful, so it's essential that I take breaks and do other things, otherwise, I just wind up frustrated.

Life is a holistic endeavor; like a giant puzzle where each piece is needed to form the whole picture. Sometimes it's hard to find the right piece, so you move on to a different section for a while. With that section done, the piece you were searching for reveals itself. Who knows, perhaps when I'm done with this book, *he* will arrive.

I'm also in an in-between stage when it comes to my personal fitness. After losing about eighteen pounds from where I was two years ago, I realized that I put about five pounds back on, mostly from not paying attention. I always find it easier to eat light in the summer months, and it's now winter, the temperature has hovered around ten degrees all week, and all I want to do is eat and sleep. I'm in my forties and my metabolism just isn't what it used to be. But to focus on my imperfections is to create a cruel-time.

Nobody has a perfect life. No one has everything in place at all times. You are always going to be in an in-between time with something, but it seems like the meantime does come in phases where there are more major ones than others.

"Don't you think you should have everything in place before you go telling people how to create their best life script," says my inner film critic, Pia. "I mean, who are *you* to talk?"

As you know, there's a season where you plant seeds, a season where you allow things to grow, and then there's the harvest. There's also the long winter, where everything appears to be dead, but it's really just in hibernation—in its resting stage. So what do you do in the meantime? How do you stay centered, at peace, and happy when you're in the long, cold winter stage, especially if it takes a lot longer than you expected?

You nurture yourself. You rest. Get lots of sun—that Caribbean vacation sounds good about now. You ask yourself how you can help others, and then you do it. You pay more attention to your fitness and nutrition. You write, do yoga, visualize, meditate, take classes, and form friendships.

Sometimes all it takes is a commitment to slowing down and taking inventory of what you have now. Letting go seems hard when you've got a tight grip on your dreams, but once you do, life gets a heck of a lot easier.

If you're anxious or depressed, connect to your source. If you're channeling Veruca Salt or feeling victimized by life, get out and go do something.

I recently decided to refocus my attention on my spiritual life. I go to a yoga class at least three times a week instead of my usual gym workouts, because I get more out of the yoga mentally and spiritually. I'm also spending more quality time with my kids. Time gets away from us. I find that focusing only on the future can distract me from the love I have here and now. I'm investing more time in my social life, meeting with friends over a glass of wine or a cup of coffee. Sometimes I am at peace doing nothing—or knitting, which centers me.

You can look to all our movie heroes and heroines for inspiration by thinking about how they spent their in-between times. Dorothy formed new friendships, Daniel fell in love with Julia in his afterlife, Scarlett became a savvy business woman, Amanda and Iris went on a vacation and learned to live in the moment and honor themselves more, Prince Albert/King George found a new, life-long friend, Phil learned to connect with his fellow man, speak French, and play piano, Charlie had fun, and Micky got a girlfriend.

I think what made the church scene in *The Color Purple* so inspiring was that Celie was between leaving Mister and seeing her sister again; Shug between finding inner peace and reuniting with her father, her church, and her children; and Alphonso was between realizing that his controlling, misogynistic behavior had caused his lonely life and doing something good by reuniting Nettie with Celie. The church scene symbolized everyone going from being spiritually disconnected (the juke joint) to connecting to their spiritual source (the church).

Celie's challenge was low self-worth and fear that she couldn't survive in the world. She barely allowed herself to dream of anything better. If she received any inspiration, it was dead as soon as it hit her sixth chakra. Her transformation involved allowing herself to imagine reuniting with her sister again, finding her voice, standing up to her abuser, connecting to her heart by loving herself, shutting out negative thoughts, embracing her inner wisdom to develop the self-confidence to leave, expressing her creativity by designing and sewing her own pants and making a living at it, and finding the courage to change her life. She stepped into her role as the lead character in her life story, and wrote a new life script where she stood center stage, surrounded by respectful, loving supporting players.

In the script at the beginning of this chapter, perhaps what the author was trying to say is that it pisses God off when we don't listen. Maybe you don't believe in God, or maybe you don't define God as others do. It doesn't matter. The best way to manage the in-between times is by slowing down, connecting to your source, going within, seeing all the wonderful things you have in your life now, cultivating patience, looking at your life, your thoughts, and your beliefs, and opening up to the possibility that perhaps some of those need to change. Choose faith over fear, and view the meantime as a verb: the time where you set your intentions and then let go and notice all the simple things that bring you joy.

Celie went years as a single woman before finally seeing her sister again, but in the meantime she started a business, surrounded herself with friends and family, and took notice of the simple things in life, even something as down-to-earth and seemingly inconsequential as the color purple.

Celie's Transformation

ACT 2

Mind
Decides she is worthy

Heart
Loves herself

Courage
Leaves abuser

ACT 1

ACT 3

Challenge:
Living with abuse, low
self-esteem

Resolution:
Happy Life

Summary

Like everyone else, I sometimes get impatient and anxious. I feel discouraged. I wonder if what I'm doing is the right thing or if what I want will ever happen. I question myself. I fear failure. I wish I had done certain things differently. I want things that seem just out of reach.

But I look around me and continue to find evidence that I *have* scripted my life, and I continue to do so. What I have now is the result of what I've scripted in the past. What's to come will be based on the story I write now, in conjunction with the divine. I just need to trust the process of life, and believe that along the way I will *know*.

What brings me peace when I experience disappointment is my belief that whatever happens is in my highest and best good and that God has a plan for me. If something doesn't work out, I may be able to look back and find things I could have done differently, but I don't live in regret. I do my best to learn the lesson, forgive myself, forgive others, and believe that what's meant to be, will be. I believe that earth is our school of life. No one is perfect. We aren't meant to be. We aren't meant to get it right every time. Olympic athletes are imperfect. Successful businesspeople are flawed. Even spiritual gurus go through divorce, illness, and disappointment.

Accept your Oscar is about being receptive to life. As you give yourself over to this process of starring in your own life story by:

- embracing your inner screenwriter,
- connecting with the light side of your character's archetypes,
- tapping in to your creative side and honoring yourself by becoming a producer,
- remaining aware of the disempowering thoughts that come

from your inner film critic and choosing instead to listen to your inner film director for guidance,

- being the protagonist in your own life story,
- having a voice in your relationships by learning your assertive lines,
- surrounding yourself with supporting players,
- setting the stage for your life by tapping in to your intuition and your imagination,
- editing from your life those things that do not serve your story, and
- remaining unattached to the outcome,

you can lead an inspirational life that would make an audience stand up and cheer, and possibly receive even better than you had imagined.

Life gives us all sorts of challenges. It never ends until we leave this world. But if you can look at it like a movie and bravely walk your path through your second act, you'll find that the best of life is yet to come. It's a process that doesn't end with the first draft. You keep writing.

*Ten Steps to Starring
in Your Own Life Story*

Embrace your inner *Screenwriter*

Develop your *Character*

Become a *Producer*

Listen to your *Director*

Be the *Star*

Learn your *Lines*

Find your *Supporting Players*

Set the *Stage*

Edit your Film

Accept your *Oscar*

Notes

Notes

EPILOGUE

Return to Oz

I come across *Wizard of Oz* symbols on a regular basis, often at a time when I need a little encouragement.

Last June I was on an airplane headed to a conference in Arizona where I was supposed to speak on a panel. As feelings of self-doubt crept in, I looked to my left to see a man reading an in-flight magazine. A picture of Dorothy holding Toto was on the right-hand page.

I was on my way to see a client on the third floor of an office building a few months ago, thinking about whether or not all of this work was ever going to pay off. Right after I entered the front doors, I saw a sign for Oz Consulting.

When I was in my ex-husband's office a few weeks ago, I looked up to find a picture of the scarecrow on the back of a brochure that peeked out from between two books on a shelf. I was feeling a bit uncomfortable, but after seeing him (the scarecrow), I felt better.

These are just a few of my *Wizard of Oz* sightings. There have been many more.

Even though I believe in signs, there is a part of me that reasons it away as simple coincidence. I'm still skeptical, which I think is healthy. *It isn't a message from the Universe. It's simply a matter of my subconscious mind being attuned to these symbols. That's all.*

Like deciding you want to buy a certain car in a particular color, all of a sudden you see the car in that exact shade of blue, everywhere you go. Still, even though my inner critic would inject her self-doubt into these synchronicities, I'd feel a wave of peace come over me whenever they'd show up. It felt like validation. And after what happened to me the other day, I *know* that these truly are signs.

I attended a four-day conference in Los Angeles put on by James Malinchak, a brilliant marketer and phenomenal public speaker. My friend, Stacy Corrigan, attended, too, although she skipped the last day to visit with her sister Bambi, who lives only fifteen minutes from the hotel. Bambi picked me up after the conference to bring me back to her house, since my flight wasn't leaving until eleven o'clock that night.

Stacy sat in the passenger seat, and I sat in the back. When we arrived, Bambi entered the passcode to open the gate to her neighborhood—a community of townhouses and condominiums. The road was narrow and winding. The grounds were well landscaped with trees and other foliage. I admired a rose garden with yellow and pink flowers on one of the center islands. People who can grow roses impress me. It made me think of a rose I planted in my front yard that didn't survive. The soil wasn't right. As she drove, she described our surroundings.

"This used to be an old MGM lot. It's where they filmed *The Wizard of Oz*," Bambi said.

Stacy shot me a look. "Amy! You asked for a literal sign!" she said.

It's true. A couple nights before, I told Stacy that I needed more clarity. Sometimes I need to be hit over the head. I wanted a clear sign, not one I had to interpret. *Skip the metaphors! Please God, give it to me straight!* We couldn't believe it. That feeling of knowing flooded my chest. *Thank you*, I said silently.

I returned home, energized. Between the conference and this little "coincidence," I couldn't wait to get home to get right back to work. But I was faced with one roadblock after another. My computer wouldn't start. I was tired from flying, but I couldn't sleep. Nothing was on TV. I was wired, so I sat down and did nothing. I let myself be. I allowed myself to think.

How interesting that I was just at the place where The Wizard of Oz *was filmed. I walked on what was once the Yellow Brick Road. What are the chances?*

In her book *Wishcraft, How to Get What You Really Want*, Barbara Sher wrote about the importance of environment. Many of us grew up in homes where well-meaning parents squashed our dreams before we even had a chance to explore them. She believes that we are all born geniuses, and so do I. It's just that the vast majority of us lacked the proper environment in which we could realize our potential. Just like a rose, we all need the right soil, water, sun, air, and time to grow. If one of the ingredients is missing, we don't thrive. We wind up

> *"Imagination has given us the steam engine, the telephone, the talking machine, and the automobile, for these things had to be dreamed of before they become realities. So I believe that dreams with your eyes wide open are likely to lead to the betterment of the world."*
>
> *— L. Frank Baum.*

feeling as though we were meant for more, enter professions that are okay but not great, and tell ourselves, *That's life. I ought to feel lucky just to have a job.*

But here's the thing—not all of us are supposed to realize our genius by the time we're eighteen. We are fed the idea that to become anything in life, you have to start young. But this isn't true. Mary Kay Ash didn't start her cosmetics company until she was forty-five. Laura Ingalls Wilder was sixty-five when she wrote Little House on the Prairie. Phyllis Sues, a dancer and musician, wrote in "Loving Life at Ninety," her article for the Huffington Post, "I started my own fashion label at fifty, became a musician and learned Italian and French in my seventies, took tango and trapeze at eighty, and walked into my first yoga class at eighty-five." http://tinyurl.com/buo52wv

L. Frank Baum was known for was his ability to enchant young children with his stories of magical, faraway places. But it wasn't until he was in his forties that he became an author. Until that time, Baum held a variety of jobs. He spent some time as an actor, worked in sales in the family business, operated a general store, and managed a weekly newspaper. Children would drop by the store and stop him on the street to ask him to tell a story. Baum imagined Oz and all of the characters. He dreamed up a fantastical place where a girl went on a hero's journey. It was his mother-in-law, the suffragette, who encouraged him to write the stories down. Oz was the perfect environment for Dorothy to transform her situation. Baum's environment was the perfect place for him to become a published author. In the 1939 movie classic by MGM, Oz is only a dream. But in Baum's best-selling children's book of 1900, Oz is a real place.

You had little control over the environment you grew up in. Now that you are grown, you have the power to create an environment where your new dreams can thrive, but like Dorothy, you need support to realize them. As a coach, I love helping people who feel trapped in their jobs, stuck in career ruts, and otherwise living like fish out of water in their own lives. I love hearing their stories and helping them create such an environment. You never know what life will bring you or how much time you have left, so the only real time you have is the present. The best dreams to have are the ones when you're awake, because they are the ones that can come true.

FILMOGRAPHY

The Wizard of Oz
screenplay by Noel Langley, Florence Ryerson, and Edgar Allan Woolf
Novel by L. Frank Baum

Defending Your Life
screenplay by Albert Brooks

Cujo
screenplay by Don Carlos Dunaway and Lauren Currier
Novel by Stephen King

Mirror, Mirror
screenplay by Marc Klein and Jason Keller

Snow White and the Huntsman
screenplay by Evan Daugherty, John Lee Hancock,
and Hossein Amini

Pretty Woman
screenplay by J. F. Lawton

Erin Brokovich
screenplay by Susannah Grant

Twilight
screenplay by Melissa Rosenberg
Novel by Stephenie Meyer

Gone with the Wind
screenplay by Sidney Howard
Novel by Margaret Mitchell

A Beautiful Mind
screenplay by Akiva Goldsman

The Holiday
screenplay by Nancy Meyers

The King's Speech
screenplay by David Seidler

Groundhog Day
screenplay by Danny Rubin

Willie Wonka and the Chocolate Factory
screenplay by Roald Dahl

The Fighter
screenplay by Scott Silver, Paul Tamasy, and Eric Johnson

The Color Purple
screenplay by Menno Meyjes
Novel by Alice Walker

For more movie credits, visit http://www.imbd.com

RECOMMENDED RESOURCES

Ahlers, Amy. *Big Fat Lies Women Tell Themselves, Ditch Your Inner Critic and Wake Up Your Inner Superstar.* 2011 New World Library.

Arewa, Caroline Shola. *Opening to Spirit, Contacting the Healing Power of the Chakras & Honouring African Spirituality.* 1998, Thorsons, London.

Arylo, Christine. *Madly in Love with Me, The Daring Adventure of Becoming Your Own Best Friend.* 2012 New World Library.

Byrne, Rhonda. *The Secret.* 2006 Atria Books.

Corrigan, Stacy. *Manifest your Man, Unlock the Secret to Bring Love into Your Life.* 2012 by Stacy Corrigan.

Hartley, Bill and Ann, editors. *The Secret Law of Attraction as Explained by Napoleon Hill.* 2008 by Highroads Media, Inc.

Hicks, Esther and Jerry. *Manifest Your Desires, 365 Ways to Make Your Dreams a Reality.* 2008 Hay House.

Jackson, Catrice M. *The Art of Fear-Free Living, Awaken your Geni(us).* 2001 by Catrice Jackson.

Judith, Anodea. *The Chakra System, A Complete Course in Self-Diagnosis and Healing.* 2003 Sounds True.

Ricco, Cia and Rosenblum, Belinda. *Self-Worth to Net Worth, 12 Keys to Creating Wealth Inside and Out.* 2012 by Rich Life Publishing.

Myss, Caroline. *Anatomy of the Spirit, The Seven Stages of Power and Healing.* 1997 Hay House.

Myss, Caroline. *Archetype Cards, An 80-Card Deck with Instruction Booklet.* 2003 Hay House.

Myss, Caroline. *Energy Anatomy, The Science of Personal Power, Spirituality, and Health.* 2001 Sounds True.

Myss, Caroline. *Sacred Contracts, Awakening Your Divine Potential.* 2001, Harmony Books.

O'Brien, Amy Beth. *Stuck with Mr. Wrong? Ten Steps to Starring in Your Own Life Story.* 2010 Bright Red Cardinal Press.

Saradananda, Swami. *The Essential Guide to Chakras, Discover the Healing Power of Chakras for Mind, Body and Spirit.* 2011 Watkins Publishing, London.

www.ingramcontent.com/pod-product-compliance
Lightning Source LLC
Chambersburg PA
CBHW060003100426
42740CB00010B/1376